GUNDOG
SOS

GUNDOG SOS

Laura Hill

THE CROWOOD PRESS

CONTENTS

PREFACE

The idea for *Gundog SOS* was born from my experience over the years of training a large variety of dogs, and working with handlers to help them get the best from their gundogs. Whilst most of the owners understood the basic principles and timeline of gundog training, and many had methodical plans to achieve their goals, there were still inevitable hiatuses in training where their own particular dog didn't fit the blueprint and progress was slow or non-existent. Some of these trainers lamented that videos and books always show things done perfectly, with the dogs doing what they should, and nothing ever going wrong. But they rarely showed problem dogs, or what to do when there were major issues or a breakdown in training.

Whilst choosing a well-bred puppy from established working lines will give owners the potential starting material to make training more straightforward, it is no guarantee of success. And when you add in human factors, it is easy to see how things can go wrong. When this happens, for some it can leave feelings of self-doubt in your ability as a trainer, and also of dread in having to take the dog out, only for issues to continue recurring.

In *Gundog SOS* I have gathered together some of the things I have learnt over the years, including wisdom from other trainers, along with knowledge and techniques that can be of use. The book doesn't contain all the answers, but instead provides an approach to avoiding some of the pitfalls in the first place, and a toolkit of ideas that can be employed to rectify some of the most common issues.

In Part I: Prevention is Better than Cure, I address some of the common mistakes made during the training process, and how we perceive some behaviours as being inherently bad. I look at when, and if, rehoming is a sensible option, and how we can change our own behaviour and strategies to find a way forwards and obtain more consistent outcomes. Reading through this first section may help you to prevent future mistakes, and help you to review your mindset with regard to undesired behaviour as it occurs. Acknowledging your own failings as well as analysing so-called problem behaviours in your dogs will also help to prevent any further deterioration in the training partnership.

In Part II: Gundog Training Clinic, we look at the more common problems seen in training, broken down by category. Case studies illustrate some of the key issues and show how these can be successfully resolved, and the chapters contain exercises and drills to improve on specific areas of weakness. Hopefully you won't have all of the common issues outlined, but some of them may resonate. You can dip into this section to help with some of the problems as they arise.

My decision to start work on this book coincided with the arrival of a pup named Vera, to whom nothing came easily. Although I would consider myself an experienced trainer, I am not afraid to admit that she was a challenge to train, and at times tested my problem-solving skills to their limit. In addition I had a young Cocker Spaniel, Purl, in training too. This was a new departure for me, taking me out of my comfort zone of retrievers, and helping me to develop new skill sets and approaches. And then along came Labrador Twig, my 'project dog', acquired at sixteen months old and definitely not a blank canvas. These three dogs have taught me a lot in the past couple of years, not just about training, but also about an approach to life.

INTRODUCTION

When you start training your gundog, you normally have some sort of expectations or a goal in mind. For example, you may be training a spaniel to accompany you rough shooting, a retriever to join you on the peg, or you may even aspire to compete with your dog. In most cases you will have started off with the blank canvas of a young puppy with a good working pedigree, and be full of hope about the bright future that lies in front of you both. However, your expectations of what the partnership between you and your dog will bring may not be realistic, or they may begin to change as issues start to occur in training that you really don't know how to rectify.

You may have read some books, done some courses, or watched DVDs and online videos of professional trainers in action. All these will likely have shown you how things should or can be done in the 'right' way, but none of them will have prepared you for what to do when things don't go to plan, or when your dog doesn't follow the expected route map, for any number of reasons.

Gundog training, like life, is rarely perfect like this, and yet some aspire to achieve perfection or even, unrealistically, to expect it. This can lead to setting goals that are impossible to achieve, resulting in dissatisfaction and frustration.

New puppies promise the start of an exciting training journey.

Early conditioning with young dogs will pay dividends later.

And whilst we use the word 'training' liberally, it is useful here to consider the semantics. Is it training or is it teaching? When you are imparting primary skills to young dogs, you are teaching or schooling them. It is very much like a child being in a classroom. Lessons can be broken down into topics, and you are imparting knowledge and techniques to help build the dog's skill set. But when we talk about training, particularly in groups, this is more akin to sports training – like going to football practice. Here, the attendees are already familiar with the rules of the game, or should be, and they are there to rehearse and practise their skills, refining them in a group context away from home. Training, in this respect, is more about using the knowledge that you have already and applying it in context.

When things go wrong, it is most commonly because the teaching or learning part, usually done at home, hasn't been consistent or thorough and there are therefore gaps in the dog's understanding. When the dog is subsequently put into a 'training session', it is poorly equipped to deal with the challenges put in front of it.

REALISTIC EXPECTATIONS

If you set perfection as your ultimate goal then it is likely that you will set yourself up for failure, because perfection in gundog training is not attainable. The bar is impossibly high if you are aiming for perfection, and small mistakes will feel like huge setbacks in reaching this target. Instead of thinking about perfection, it is perhaps more helpful to think about excellence instead, which is still about achieving greatness or brilliance, but allows you to accept mistakes and embrace failure as part of the process, and to learn from it. Excellence is rarely achieved 'first time out'. It takes a lot of practice and learning along the way.

If you are struggling in your gundog journey, try to take the pressure off yourself by acknowledging that it is enough to make an effort and be 'good enough' at some things along the way. This doesn't mean accepting substandard work forever, but understanding that doing your best as you go along is a more positive approach. This will improve your enjoyment of the process and offers you a kinder self-dialogue instead of a harsh or self-judging one. It is also a way of overcoming procrastination, as it is less daunting making a start. Put your time and effort into becoming better at training and understanding the learning process. This is empowering and will help you reach your aspirations.

A STITCH IN TIME

When you notice that an issue has crept into your training, it is rarely a good idea to ignore it or to hope that it will improve on its own over time. Quite often handlers will say 'he's just a puppy', and this can be a good catch-all phrase to excuse undesirable or juvenile behaviour. Of course, genuine puppy behaviour on the part of very young dogs that haven't been taught, or that haven't learnt what is expected of them in different circumstances, is totally accept-

able. But it is when the behaviour becomes ingrained into a pattern that is undesirable in the long term that it needs addressing. In this respect, as the saying goes, 'a stitch in time saves nine'. Acknowledging the problem behaviour and setting up a plan to deal with it in a timely manner will mean that it is easier to rectify and doesn't become something that is unfixable at a later date.

The golden period of the first six to seven months in the puppy's life is the most important period to imprint good habits whilst it is still very impressionable, so that it is set up for what is expected in later training. However, with a good plan in place there is still the opportunity to set things right at a later date, if you haven't been able to capitalise on this early training time.

Find a trusted mentor who makes you feel comfortable.

CHOOSING A TRAINER

In the real world, things don't always go to plan. You may have inherited a legacy of problems, or created some habits that you don't want, in which case it is time to seek some help. Many people will have realised that they have some significant issues with their gundog, but will wait until after the shooting season has finished before seeking professional help. If this is the case, ensure that your dog (and you) have had an adequate break before you turn your attention to some remedial spring/summer training. This may mean planning regular sessions with a local trainer to give you a framework to your training plan, or it might be booking some 'away days' to give your dog experience of new grounds, or yourself some input from a different training professional.

But how do you go about finding the right training, or rather the right trainer, for you? Choosing the perfect trainer can be tricky, especially if you don't have personal knowledge of individuals and their style. In this case it pays to do some research, or at least to ask around. When you do find a trainer whom you think might fit your needs, don't be frightened to ask them some questions (*see* box).

Once you have chosen a trainer, and a style of training that suits you, you will need to ensure that your goals and expectations are in line. There are rarely any instant cures in gundog training, so an ethical trainer should be honest and help you set reasonable expectations. It may be that you are looking to 'fix' some issues that have crept in, or that you just want ongoing routine training. As a rule, if you have a retriever, you are far better going to a trainer who specialises in retrievers rather than someone who works mainly with spaniels or hunt, point and retrieve dogs (HPRs), as there are nuances in training for the different sub-groups. In addition, if you have a specific issue, try to find someone who has worked with that specific issue and has documented success.

One of the most important things to consider when you are working with a trainer is whether they make you feel comfortable. They will be working with you, not just assessing the dog, so ensuring that you are confident and at ease with the person training you and your dog is very important. You should be able to trust them and approach them with questions or ask for suggestions that are appropriate for you. In turn, they should be able to be honest with you, rather than just massaging your ego.

It is acceptable to be selective about who trains you. A good trainer will be happy to talk to you about any questions that you have relating to their style of training.

THE QUALITIES OF A GOOD COACH

If you are lucky, on your gundog journey you will come across, and be guided by, a really good trainer. And if you are even more fortunate, then that trainer may become a trusted mentor or coach. Teaching is a skill like any other, but there are some who are able to get their message across more powerfully, or inspire and channel a wide range of students, pushing them beyond their comfort zones and moving them on to achieve higher goals.

Great coaches are perceptive and patient, and can tease out the relevant information from their students. They help fuel and direct individual growth, using their knowledge and ability to recognise issues. They also connect with their students to deliver relevant support in a meaningful way. A great coach is not only wise, but has the ability to communicate that wisdom to move their students forwards, and often beyond their own comfort zones. In this way, the coach should be able to look deeper at issues and scenarios, applying their own relevant experience, which has often been built up over many decades, and also their creativity to problem solve. And whilst technical knowledge is paramount, gundog training is also about 'feel' and the art. A gundog trainer may know how to teach the basic mechanical skills of handling and hunting their dog, but learning to read live situations (wind direction, terrain factors, canine and human body language, handler emotions, behavioural science) adds a whole additional layer to the basic technical skills.

What are your methods?

Why did the trainer choose these methods, and why do they work? Are they the same for every client, or do they vary? A good trainer should be able to explain their methods clearly, and also the science and reasoning behind them.

What are your ethics?

The trainer should be able to explain their feelings and the reasoning behind their methods, and what their priorities are during training.

What is your background and experience?

Does the trainer have any certification, or any type of formal education in teaching or animal behaviour? Are they members of, or affiliated to any organisations? Some gundog trainers will have taken professional courses in general dog training. Others won't have this, but may have vast experience in the shooting or competition field. If you are specifically seeking preparation for competitions such as field trials, find out if they have a proven track record in this area, and a full understanding of the requirements for success. If you are visiting a trainer for help with a particular issue, make sure the trainer has suitable experience with the specific area with which you need help.

What are your prices and availability?

Do some research to ensure that the price is fair, considering their background, expertise and facilities. Also, factor in any travel time to get there. Would online lessons work for you, or do you need face-to-face help? If you are looking for an ongoing relationship with the trainer, make sure that they can meet your needs for continued support. You may only want an assessment and suggestions for homework, or you might need ongoing help via regular lessons.

Do you have customer testimonials or feedback?

Personal recommendations are invaluable here, if you don't know the trainer. But beware on-line reviews from people you don't know. If the trainer doesn't have any reviews, find out if they are happy to refer you to other clients to provide references.

In this respect, the coach needs to be extremely perceptive, and to represent a 'fresh pair of eyes' on your partnership. But it is more than that. It is hard to see yourself and your dog from an objective position sometimes. You get wrapped up in your own habits, which are often deeply ingrained. A great coach has a sharpness and perceptiveness that goes beyond just regarding the handler and their dog. They will see another layer, or pick out a particular detail. They will notice subtle aspects or differences. They get to know their students, analysing them and their dogs, and will customise their communications to fit that particular pairing. They should be curious and investigative. If you get the opportunity to observe a good trainer giving a lesson, you will see them watching and analysing not only what the dogs are doing, but what the handlers are doing too – unpicking tiny details and asking questions.

From these perceptions will come the timely delivery of relevant information. This can be a commentary as a particular retrieve unfolds, or an analysis after the event, with accurate observations and suggestions. And whilst some coaches are seen to have great patience, it is more than this: it is actually more of a probing impatience, which strategically unpicks various aspects of behaviour. The coach will be on hand to offer one strategy, but will also be ready with a plan B if the first idea doesn't work.

Good coaches engage with their students, providing honest feedback and ongoing support.

And they will have an arsenal of suggestions by way of advice, and other options available to employ. And once a student is consistently achieving certain tasks then the good coach will be ready to move them on and deliver new layers of information to increase their overall skill, pushing them beyond their sweet spot and on towards greater achievement. Whilst small successes are acknowledged and applauded along the way, they are not seen as stopping points, but rather as steps up towards the next level.

A good coach should not only be able to engage with you, but should also adjust their style to suit your needs at the time. Sometimes 'tough love' is appropriate, sometimes a more nurturing approach is necessary. Some students need frank feedback, whereas others want patient support. Great teachers understand those differing needs and can connect empathetically with their students. They allow their students to figure out some things for themselves, which will develop their problem-solving capacity and eventually make them more independent. They won't spoonfeed their pupils, but will give them homework and ask them to go away and work on the areas that need improvement, making some mistakes along the way as part of the learning process.

Finally, 'character' is perhaps the secret ingredient of many good coaches. The possession of an analytical mind paired with wit or good humour goes a long way to inspire students further towards their goals.

LISTENING

This might seem a strange topic to include in a gundog training book, but it is a skill that is vital to handlers as they seek to improve their dog's (and their own) capabilities. Listening is an important and fundamental component of your interpersonal communication skills. It is not something that just happens – that is hearing. It is, or should be, an active process, when a conscious decision is made to listen to and understand the messages of the speaker. How well you listen can have a major impact on your effectiveness as a handler and trainer, and also on the quality of your relationships with others.

Listening is important for several reasons, namely:

- to obtain information
- to understand instructions
- for enjoyment
- to learn more

Given all the listening that humans do in daily life, you would think we'd be good at it! However, most of us are not, and it is thought that we only remember less than 50 per cent of what we hear, which means that when you talk to your friends, colleagues, clients or spouse for ten minutes, they will probably only pay attention to around three minutes of that conversation. Turn this around and it reveals that, when you are being presented with information, you are unlikely to listen to the whole message either. You hope the important parts are captured in the small percentage that you did retain, but this may not be the case.

Improving Your Listening Skills

Clearly, listening is a skill that we can all benefit from improving. By becoming a better listener, you can increase your productivity, as well as your ability in turn to train and influence. You will also avoid frustration and misunderstanding, which is necessary for successful outcomes.

The way to improve your listening skills is to practise 'active listening'. This is where you make a conscious effort to hear not only the words that another person is saying, but also, and more importantly, the entire message that is being communicated. In order to do this you must pay attention to the other person very carefully. You cannot allow yourself to become distracted by whatever else may be going on around you, or by forming counter arguments while the other person is still speaking. Nor should you get bored and lose focus on what they are saying. Have you ever been in a training group where other handlers are talking to each other rather than listening to the trainer, or browsing on their smartphones? It is hard to maintain focus for a prolonged period of time, so this behaviour is accepted. But bear this in mind when you think about your dog's focus during that session as well.

Active listening is a skill that can be acquired and developed with practice. However, it can be difficult to master, and will therefore take time and patience to develop. As its name suggests, it is taking part in the listening process: that is, fully concentrating on what is being said rather than just passively hearing the message of the speaker.

It involves listening with all the senses. As well as giving full attention to the speaker, you should try to show that you are listening by using both verbal and non-verbal signals, such as maintaining eye

TECHNIQUES OF ACTIVE LISTENING

- Smiling
- Eye contact
- Nodding
- Posture – leaning slightly forwards or having a slight head slant
- Mirroring – reflecting facial expressions
- Use of positive reinforcement via marker words
- Asking questions, clarifying
- Vocal reflection – repeating things
- Summarising or paraphrasing what has been said

Use active listening techniques to help you remember information.

contact, nodding your head and smiling, or agreeing by saying 'yes', 'right' or simply 'ah ha' to encourage them to continue. By providing this feedback, the person speaking will usually feel more at ease and will therefore communicate more readily and openly. To understand the importance of active listening, ask yourself if you've ever been engaged in a conversation when you weren't sure if the other person was listening to what you were saying. You will have wondered if your message was getting across, or if it was even worthwhile continuing to talk.

If you find it difficult to concentrate on what a trainer is saying to you, try repeating some of their words after they have said them, silently in your head. This will help to reinforce the key points and help you to retain focus. You can also make notes, either into a digital voice recorder on your phone or in a pocket notebook.

The ability to listen to and analyse information and then put this learning into practice will go a long way towards making your training more efficient and meaningful.

1 MISTAKES

To Err is human.

ALEXANDER POPE, 1711

When things go wrong, it is very often down to human error. For example, if you analyse the true cause of most modern-day aircraft crashes, you will see that the majority were caused by human factors, and very few by aircraft technical faults. Humans are fallible. We make the wrong decisions or choices, fail to act in a timely manner, or don't communicate our intentions to others. Gundog training is no different in this respect.

Making mistakes or one-off 'bloopers' is fine. It is only when these are repeated that it becomes an issue. If you make an error in training that leads to some sort of failure, try not to let it happen again and move on. You will need to accept failure and get used to it as being part of the overall training process. This will apply not only in training but also in competition. Failure is inevitable at some point, but it should also be seen as a positive force in that it can lead to adaptation and innovation.

When mistakes are made, use this as an opportunity to get creative and try new things to solve the issues. If you think of the scientist in a laboratory where an experiment didn't turn out as planned, this is often the route to new discoveries. For example, it was only when Sir Alexander Fleming threw away a contaminated petri dish that he noticed that the mould growing in it was destroying bacteria. This led him to his discovery of penicillin. And the microwave oven was inadvertently invented by Percy Spencer, who realised that his confectionary bar was melting during his radar-related experiments with a new vacuum tube device.

There is usually an opportunity to learn from mistakes, so get comfortable with them. Try different approaches to resolve problems. Some will work and some won't. However, try to avoid multiple failures. After something has gone wrong, try to reset for success. This means excluding the conditions for failure so that it doesn't happen again, and this may mean lowering the criteria or simplifying the exercise. Try to set up the conditions so that it would be impossible for the same behaviour to happen again.

When dogs get things wrong, or don't behave as we would hope, it is usually down to a failure on our own part. There are a number of common mistakes that trainers make, which result in a breakdown in understanding on the dog's part, and consequently poor performance.

POOR COMMUNICATION AND TIMING

Quite often the dog simply does not understand what is required of it. This may be because you haven't communicated effectively what you want in an appropriate way. For example, shouting 'get over, get over' at a dog that is running up and down a fence line to try to make it jump over the fence will not work unless you have actually taught the dog that 'get over' means jump. In fact, what you are actually inadvertently doing is labelling the behaviour of fence running, if you do this repeatedly. Some handlers think that the dog will automatically understand the meaning of the words, but this is not the case. The 'get over' cue would need to be chained, and proofed, to

If the cue is not thoroughly conditioned, the dog will not understand that you want him to jump the fence.

the act of jumping over a fence and other obstacles.

As well as ensuring that your communication is clear, you need to work hard to ensure your feedback to the dog is timely. This is one of the most common problems that novice handlers struggle with – when to praise or correct, and the ability to move quickly between the two responses. Getting your timing right is critical, otherwise you can end up inadvertently rewarding a behaviour that you don't want. Equally, withholding praise for good work can be a mistake if you have other issues that you want to address with remediation.

Sometimes the cues that you give to the dog can be confusing. These may be intentional or unintentional: for example, your intention is to direct the dog to go right handed, but before you push right, you actually swing your arm over your head momentarily leftwards. The dog then goes left, and the handler is annoyed, as in their view they gave a clear right-hand cast. However, the dog has acted quickly on the (unintentional) cue to move left, and the handler construes this as defiance or naughtiness.

At other times, mistimed praise can lead to continued undesired behaviour. Many handlers are quick

Take care to make your arm signals clear.

to praise their dog with 'good boy' when it finds the dummy, but don't notice that the dog is actually briefly hunting on before returning whilst being praised. The handler has now rewarded the dog for hunting on when that wasn't his intention – but the dog understands that this behaviour is not only acceptable but now doubly rewarding.

RUSHING

The foundations for successful gundog work are the core skills of heelwork, stays/steadiness and recall. These are not the most interesting or rewarding tasks to teach, either for dog or handler, and often they end up being glossed over or rushed in order to get on with the more interesting retrieve or hunting work.

One of the most common mistakes in training is to miss things out, or only partially teach the skills necessary. This will eventually lead to confusion for the dog as there will be gaps in its understanding and education. Trying to do too much, too quickly for the dog is likely to end up in frustration when that plan doesn't work. Instead, a methodical step-by-step approach should be applied, whereby you only

Reward the puppy for incremental changes in behaviour to speed its learning.

move on to the next stage once the previous stage is completed. This requires a degree of self-discipline.

Trainers who are familiar with the concept of clicker training will have an advantage here, as they work at noticing and rewarding small increments of behaviour change. The dog receives lots of very small 'wins' along the way to reaching the eventual fully-shaped desired behaviour. The important aspect is not upping the criteria too quickly to get to your goal. For example, if you want a young puppy to sit on a placeboard that he has never seen before, you would firstly click and reward the dog for just being near the board. Next, you might withhold the click until the dog looks at the board. Then you might click when the dog puts his nose on the board. After that you could wait so you only click when the dog places a paw on the board, and so on. Until eventually, after several sessions, you will have a puppy that can go and sit on the placeboard. The dog is happy to do this work as it is being rewarded for all its attempts along the way, and there is no long period when the dog is confused as to what is required.

Breaking down your training into small achievable tasks in this manner will help you to reach your larger

Heelwork is one of the most important foundations of gundog work.

Get help with larger projects and approach them in a methodical way.

A friend came over to help me clear a large pile of tree branches and brashings from the paddock, where we had felled a couple of trees. The area needed to be prepared ready to sow with cover-crop seeds. There was a huge volume of material to remove, and I had been trying to drag large branches off the ground myself and hide them in the undergrowth, but my friend suggested a fire would be better to get rid of everything properly. I was dubious that burning was going to be effective, especially when the wood was so fresh and green. But she reassured me that it would work well, and showed me how to start and build a fire effectively to create maximum heat. I was keen to learn some new skills. But what I learned along the way was not just about building fires...

Start small

The most important thing she told me was to 'start small', and I realised that this applies to how we should approach our training. Some-times training issues can seem so complex and insurmountable, and it is hard to see a way around them. Or it is difficult to contemplate teaching a dog all the things it is going to need to understand during its career as a gundog. But if we break things down and start with the very smallest of steps it is much easier to see some progress. For example, I have found training Vera extremely challenging, as she hasn't had much of a desire to return to me if she has retrieved, and then we have had delivery issues. But by breaking things down, and back-chaining small, individual tasks, these were eventually built into the full retrieve. Also, documenting this journey via videos was a great way to actually see, and analyse, if things were going in the right direction (and it had the knock-on effect of making me want to train a little more, to get a little more progress). It's rather a cliché to say 'from small acorns...' – but it really is true. Simplifying and building slowly really does provide a good way forwards.

Lay all your sticks in the same direction

This is not what an archetypal bonfire looks like! But the rationale is that when one stick finishes burning it makes way for the next to fall down into its place. And it really works. This resonated with me when thinking about training. It is important how you do things, ensuring you put your foundations in place first, but also making sure that things fit together logically – no going off at tangents or making things unnecessarily complicated. Burn through one stick and then move on to the next.

Controlled burning

You don't want a raging inferno. When something is burning well, there's no need to add more fuel to it (in fact our fire was started without any sort of fire accelerant other than a tiny fire lighter). Just monitor the burning and gradually add more sticks to keep it going.

The tendency to rush things and keep piling things on can lead to things getting out of control quickly.

Get help

Most of the time we can cope on our own, and this is satisfactory. But sometimes getting help really is needed and appreciated, whether that is through a professional trainer, friend or partner. Doing things in company can just make things more pleasant – and it helps with motivation, too. And the shared feeling of collective achievement is very uplifting. If you can't see the wood for the trees, then a fresh pair of eyes or new approach can make all the difference, and in some cases can be revolutionary.

goals. Using a method such as a checklist, where you tick off a certain number of repetitions of a key task, is a simple way of ensuring that you don't rush through the core skills, and that you have done an adequate number of rehearsals of these behaviours before moving on to more complex tasks. It is also a very satisfying way of achieving little wins. For example, with a young dog I might start the process of teaching her to 'lock on' when I throw a mark. This means holding her visual focus on the dummy when it lands and keeping that focus until she is sent. With my checklist approach to training, all I have to do is go out and practise my 'locking on' exercise once a day for four days out of seven. I will tick off each time I have done this task, and I might make comments on how the dog is relating to the exercise. Progress is made this way, simply through repetition.

FAILURE TO PROOF BEHAVIOURS

Once each step has been trained at home (both in the house and garden), then it is necessary to take these core behaviours to different locations, and proof them under a variety of conditions so that the behaviour is generalised. Failure to do this will mean that the dog's behaviour is unreliable when it is taken to different grounds. How often have you heard the expression (or even used it yourself): 'He's never done that before!'? This is often said when handlers are surprised that their dog has not done something that they are sure they have already taught it. However, the dog has not been trained to carry out this behaviour in this particular location, and that is key here. For example, retrieving at home, alone, in the garden, is a very different activity to retrieving in the company of other dogs in a field that has long grass with pheasant and deer scent in it.

Your dog may have a great foundation of general obedience behaviours when you are training alone, but taking it into a group can be a whole other experience, and sometimes handlers can be very dismayed and disappointed when they realise that the learning has not yet been adequately generalised. After

TRAINING FOMO (FEAR OF MISSING OUT)

Social media has been both a blessing and a curse with respect to gundog training in groups. We are now able to see friends and fellow trainers across the country or even across the world, training in some breathtaking venues and on extreme terrains. Across the UK there are several purpose-built commercial grounds now used specifically for gundog training, which offer a wide variety of features such as lakes, streams, fences, walls, ditches, moorland and various cover crops. Access to interesting land to train on is increasingly readily available. And when you see people sending their dogs for long-distance challenging retrieves, incorporating multiple factors or barriers, it is difficult to resist wanting to have a go yourself, too. Many fear that by staying at home they might be missing out. But if your dog is not already well trained and able to handle reliably, then it will be ill equipped for such distances and demands. Then instead of being beneficial, this sort of training excursion can actually have a detrimental effect on your overall long-term training.

Whilst it is very gratifying to see your dog run out vast distances, you do need to consider what your long-term goals are in undertaking these retrieves, and also what you will do if it doesn't go to plan.

Will the experience be confidence boosting or confidence sapping? Are you practising success or rehearsing failure? Over-facing young dogs can have a very detrimental effect. To undertake this sort of training you should ensure that your dog has a reasonable 'stop', and that he will handle at distance, so the retrieve doesn't fall apart. Also, the dog should have a more-than-average level of fitness to cope both physically and mentally on such testing terrain.

It is tempting to want to go on training trips because friends or fellow trainers are undertaking these. But you should consider what would be in the best interest of training your own dog at this particular stage in its career. Sometimes staying at home and working on basic handling and drill exercises will pay dividends over the seemingly more glamorous excursions to distant venues. In this respect, staying at home may actually put you in a more advantageous position.

Training trips away offer new experiences for handler and dog, but ensure your dog is well prepared for the challenges.

doing your foundation work alone at home, the next step would be to take these behaviours to different locations, again alone, and practise them, ensuring that the dog is working reliably under the different conditions. Next you should try to pair up with another handler and go through these same behaviours in each other's company, firstly on home ground again and then on the other grounds you have visited. Once you feel confident that the dog's behaviour is reliable under these conditions, you can then take it into a group setting – but be prepared to lower your expectations of the dog, and simplify the work you ask it to do so that you are setting it up for success.

FATIGUE

Fatigue can be a big factor both for the handler and the dog. If you are working alone, keep your training sessions short. Retrieves can soon mount up with a single dog, and the temptation is to carry on doing just a bit more.

Factor in the dog's age and their stage of training, also how long their attention span is, as well as their overall level of fitness. With a young pup, both their mind and joints are not yet fully formed, so sessions really should be kept brief.

When things start to go wrong, particularly towards the end of a session, it is usually never a good idea to battle on through this. Try to recognise training fatigue and take a break. Stop the session short on something the dog can achieve easily, and make a note to return to the exercise another day. This is usually far better than trying to push on through the problem when you risk compounding an issue or making a negative association with the whole exercise.

Handler tiredness and state of mind should also be factored in. If you don't really feel like going out training, but feel you ought to, then don't. It rarely ends well. Go for a nice walk together instead, and pick another day to train when you are in a better frame of mind.

FRUSTRATION

Again, frustration can be felt by both the handler and the dog. Try to make the training tasks achievable for your dog. Occasionally you will want to 'stretch' the dog to see what stage it is at, but if everything is too hard or complicated then this will lead to frustration, which may be manifested in different ways. Some dogs will shut down and not be able to continue in their work, whilst others will become increasingly manic, appearing to rush around in a 'headless' manner as they try to solve the problem with physical effort rather than by using their brain.

For the handler, if you feel you are getting frustrated with the dog it is probably time either to stop, or to back-pedal. Review how realistic your expectations are of the dog in this particular situation: 'But he knows this!' It may be a change in the ground that is having an impact, different training companions, the weather, or a combination of all these factors. In which case, simplify what you are asking him in order to consolidate what he does know, and to relieve the pressure on him, and the feelings of frustration.

Tiredness leads to lack of concentration. Keep training sessions short.

MAKING COMPARISONS

Many people will have been to puppy classes with their new puppies, and met puppies of a similar age to their own. And others may have been in these same classes alongside litter mates to their own puppies. It is interesting to see how your pup compares. It is human nature and natural curiosity to check our own puppy's progress against those of others. But it can also end up being slightly demoralising, and sometimes even toxic. Comparing yourself, or your dog, to others can sometimes leave you feeling substandard. As Theodore Roosevelt so rightly said: 'Comparison is the thief of joy.'

You may have been working on your foundation behaviours at home, and been happy with how your new pup is progressing and picking things up. You have found that he is bright and a source of pride and joy, not only in your choice of good breeding, but in your prowess as a trainer. Some things have gone well, and others have been more of a struggle, but you are making your own way. And then you get into a training group, and all of a sudden you feel as if your pup is 'bottom of the class', or just not quite as bright a star as you had originally believed.

These group classes are excellent for proofing core behaviours that you have been working on at home. But they are not always the best for your own self-esteem and confidence if things do not go to plan. And sometimes this can lead to anxiety when you feel that your pup is not measuring up, or a feeling of envy when you see what some of the others can do in comparison. And although you have been taught that it is 'stage, not age' with puppy training, it is very hard not to measure your puppy against the milestones of others.

Natural Traits

Some comparison is good, and it can be rewarding and enlightening – for example when you observe litter siblings and some of their genetic traits and similarities. These can be physical appearances, features they have adopted from one or both parents, the way they move (running or hunting), their style and characteristics. These are things you can't really influence. However, it is useful to note the similarities and differences, and you may be able to use these observations to inform your approach to training. For example, if all the pups within a particular litter are showing signs of being voracious hunters, then you might focus your efforts on ensuring that more work is done on promoting 'run' over hunting. This desire to hunt may be a default behaviour. Likewise, if many of the littermates are less bold or are shy, then you might feel reassured that this isn't as a result of a traumatic event at home, or lack of socialisation, but rather something that is more in the character of the puppy.

Litter siblings Opal and Twig share some physical and mental attributes, but also have as many differences.

Organised competitions will highlight how your dog measures up to others in its class.

Comparison is not helpful when you are looking at the level of training that has been accomplished, because all puppies progress at different levels, and may ebb and flow in their capabilities as they age. For example some are 'slow burners', and show little desire to retrieve perhaps at an early age – then suddenly at a later date it is as if a light bulb has been switched on, and they roar away from the starting blocks at last! These puppies, that seemed unpromising, are now filled with drive and enthusiasm as they have matured. Conversely, some pups are naturally very quick to pick things up from a startlingly young age. They just progress eagerly and readily. And there is no reason to try to hold them back if they are ready to be 'stretched' a little in their training.

Trainer Influence

The other thing to consider when assessing your puppy is the experience of the owner you are comparing it against. It isn't just the pup's natural ability that has a bearing on its progress, but that in combination with how it has been trained. Some trainers are more adept than others at getting the best out of their puppies at a very young age, whereas others struggle to get to grips with the basics, or prefer to leave the pup to 'be a puppy' for a longer time. Eventually you are all heading to the same place, so it doesn't matter if the journeys are of differing lengths.

Healthy Competition

Training groups are not the place to compare your pups or even older dogs with the other participants, as this is your forum to work on building their skill sets in company, and to notice the elements that still need more attention at home; nevertheless, there are times when some comparison can be fun. That role can be fulfilled by entering organised working tests, and later on, field trials.

The competition arena is necessarily the place where you are able to compare your dog against those of others, and gain a more objective view (from qualified judges) on its overall merits. Pitching your dog against 20 or 30 others and coming away with some recognition in the way of an award can be very gratifying. It is a recognition of your own efforts in training, and also hopefully of the natural ability of your dog. It is a rewarding feeling to have your work in training endorsed by somebody else. However, it is unlikely that your dog will feel the same way! They may enjoy a nice day out with you, but win or lose, they will be equally happy to go home with you again.

PERMISSIVE MENTALITY

Early conditioning, and how you approach training, can play a key role in how the dog relates to external stimuli and how it is able to regulate its own behaviour. Rewarding the dog for 'good' choices, rather than imposing your instructions on the dog and attempting to manage its behaviour yourself, will be more useful in the long run in teaching the dog to manage its own impulses and behaviours.

This approach can be built into early routines with young puppies. For example, with a puppy housed in a crate, when the door is opened the puppy may try to barge out of the door. You might consider this to be bad manners, and prefer that the puppy waited while the door was opened and then was invited out on cue. There are two distinct ways of achieving this, but with subtle differences.

First, you could tell the dog to 'sit' or 'stay' while you open the door. This method gives the dog a command or cue for behaviour that you want him to carry out. But by doing this, you are taking control or managing the dog's behaviour. The alternative

would be that each time the dog tries to barge out of the crate you merely shut the door again, preventing the dog from making any progress in its endeavours. The dog will gradually learn that trying to rush out is futile, and so it will learn from the experience and adapt its behaviour to try to find an alternative that will enable it to progress. After rushing the gate and having it promptly shut in its face, the pup may decide to sit for a second or two to see what happens then. It has managed its own impulse to rush out, rather than being told not to do so. This behaviour is then rewarded by you opening the door and calling the dog out.

The differences here are subtle but important, and when you relate them to the field you can see the clear benefit of self-management. When you are standing at a heavy drive and you have a dog that is accustomed to managing its own impulses and regulating its own behaviour, you will feel more confident and relaxed than you would with one that you are having to continually monitor and manage yourself.

Another exercise that is useful here is to teach your dog only to take its food on your cue. So, as with the crate scenario above, when you go to put the food bowl on the floor and the dog dives towards it to eat, you would simply pick up the bowl before it was able to do so. Standing in front of the dog, lower the bowl and raise it again if the dog makes any movement. Gradually the dog will learn the 'rules of engagement' and how it should manage its own behaviour to get access to the food. Once the dog is waiting patiently you can release it on cue, using 'take it'. The important point here is that you have not asked the dog to do anything such as sit, wait or stay, but are just getting the dog to adapt its own behaviour to receive the reward.

CREATING INADVERTENT LEARNING

It is often difficult to realise that we have made mistakes in this respect. But it is an important area to consider. If you have ever been with a professional trainer they may have picked out something such as the fact that your dog is returning to heel with the dummy after a retrieve, rather than bringing it to your front. This is a subtle behaviour difference, and I have heard handlers say: 'I haven't taught him to do that. He just does it.' But of course, this behaviour has been (inadvertently) taught or learned by the fact that the dog has been reinforced for it. That is, the dog now comes directly to heel instead of to the front with the retrieve because it knows it will be sent from that position for another retrieve. It is thus far more rewarding to be sitting face out into the field than to be facing the handler.

Jumping up and then getting down again can become part of the reward chain.

This dog has learnt that the rewards come from the dummy thrower in front.

Other areas of inadvertent learning include building 'bad' behaviour chains, such as 'yo-yo' heelwork, whereby the dog is in position, then pulls forwards, out of position, but self-corrects by jumping back into position, and then receives a food reward for being back in position again. The association can quickly become that heelwork incorporates pulling forwards and jumping back and being rewarded in turn, rather than maintaining a consistent position overall for the duration of the walk. To overcome this behaviour you will need to break down the heelwork into much smaller increments, rewarding the dog whilst it is in position, first statically at heel, and then for just a single step, and so on. You should not give the dog the opportunity to pull forwards or put itself out of position. This way you will make the heel position reliable again.

Another variation of an undesirable chain of behaviour is the dog jumping up on you, then being asked to sit in front of you instead, and then being rewarded for sitting. The learning for the dog, here, is that he needs to do the jumping up behaviour first to start the chain of behaviour before the eventual reward. In this respect you need to be very careful about what you reward, and must understand where there may be linked chains of behaviour. Breaking down the behaviour into small fragments will help you to reward the desired behaviour at the time.

EXCUSES, EXCUSES

In a podcast interview, Nepalese mountaineer Nims Purja, who conquered fourteen mountain peaks (all above 8,000m) in a world record-breaking time, had a lot of inspirational input to give listeners. One of the most poignant things he said was: 'Stop making excuses: winners don't make excuses, losers do.' How very true this is. Those who compete in field trials will know that the winner's speech at the end of the day is never littered with excuses about their performance or that of their dog. They don't criticise the ground or doubt the judges' decisions. But how often do you hear those who haven't quite made the grade on that day reel out a chain of excuses? Most of us have done this at some point, because it's just not palatable to accept that it is usually our own fault when we don't succeed in our endeavours.

Instead of making excuses, try to be true to yourself and act with self-discipline, making yourself accountable for the things that haven't gone to plan. We all make mistakes, but we don't all have to keep repeating them. For example, when you come home from a competition such as a field trial or working test, try to record a few notes about it and how it has gone. You can make a note of your place, if you get one, but also make a note of what the ground was like and how the dog (and you) performed, and what your weaknesses were. If you do this honestly, you will be able to spot patterns, and use the information to inform any future training.

NEVER GIVE UP

When issues arise that seem unsurmountable, it is very easy to become disheartened. The desire to 'give up' when things go wrong can happen both whilst training or competing. Some handlers are more resilient than others in the face of these issues. I remember when, several years ago, I was struggling to pick a tricky blind retrieve on a hare in a field trial, and my shoulders must have slumped and given away to the judge the fact that I was losing heart. I had made several casts and was feeling like giving up. He noticed this and said to me 'Never give up'. I battled on to make the retrieve, and although we didn't win the stake, we did still feature in the awards. It was a lesson learnt that I continue to carry with me, namely that it is worth fighting to get results. Sometimes a struggle is necessary.

Try not to give up when you handle your dog and things don't go to plan.

1. Listen to yourself

You should have a good understanding of what is realistic and what isn't. Assess the situation. If you can't overcome a problem, then accept that and move on. Listen to your instincts. Friends will sometimes offer advice or, more usually, platitudes. Weigh up whether this advice will work for you and your own circumstances.

2. Think small

Rather than setting large, unachievable goals, and then having to make an excuse because you couldn't get there, set mini goals along the pathway. These smaller goals are much easier to achieve, and will pave your way to success. You might not be able to keep this going forever, but even just a period of concerted effort to achieve some small wins can help you along your overall gundog training journey.

3. Think possible

If others have achieved it, then it has been proved possible. Take steps to make your dream a reality.
  It's easy to say 'I could never do that!' But remember, even those professional trainers started somewhere. None of us was born a gundog trainer! It is a set of skills and practices that is acquired over time, with application and patience. Read books, watch videos, attend training classes, talk to friends and professionals, offer to help at events – these are all steps towards making it happen.

4. 'I want to...' becomes 'I'm going to...'

A change in the way we talk about our behaviour is a powerful way to propel you towards action. Make this the year that you do. Turn 'I want my dog to stop on the whistle' into 'I'm going to teach my dog to stop on the whistle.' This highlights the active role that you need to play in the process.

5. Embrace the unknown, don't fear it

Making changes may include taking some risks, but the positives from this will usually outweigh the negatives. Research and analyse to help you understand your desires. You may never have been on a training trip with your dog, tried entering a working test, or had one-to-one coaching with a professional. Is that because it sounds daunting? Or because you don't know what to expect? Use your network of training friends to help you find out more about what to expect. Ask questions, and help yourself become confident enough to have a go.

6. Stop blaming others

It's easy to make excuses and blame others for things that 'happen' to you. But it is also quite destructive, because this mindset erodes your personal power. Take control and recognise your individual responsibility. Things go wrong – often – when you train a gundog! This is not unique to you. But taking ownership actually helps you to overcome issues: knowing that you can make a change by doing something is empowering. Try to enhance your own resilience.

7. Stop comparing yourself to others

Some comparisons can be healthy if used for benchmarking, but largely they can promote negative feelings. Don't let the success of others take away from your own achievements. Another handler achieving a top place in an Open Field Trial should not detract from your own successes at a different level – whether that is finessing your delivery during training, or gaining a first award in a Novice Handler competition. Set your own personal goals, and celebrate achieving them.

Robert the Bruce, King of Scotland, is alleged to have said 'If at first you don't succeed, try, try and try again' to his troops before they successfully defeated the English in battle at Bannockburn in 1314. It is a saying that many of us will be familiar with, when faced with adversity. Along your gundog training journey there will be inevitable problems and issues, and only through perseverance will you be able to get through these. This will mean working methodically to deal with the barriers to progress as they arise.

Perseverance, and a deal of resilience, is a required trait for gundog training. The path is not always straightforward, but sticking to your training goals and principles will help you find a way through. It is no coincidence that the saying above repeats the word 'try' three times. This can be directly related to how you approach a training task that is going wrong. For example, if you are lining your dog to a particular tree to pick a retrieve, and the dog veers off course almost immediately, you can call it back to you, re-set it up, and try again. Next you send it again in the same manner, and again it goes off course. Once more you send it, and this time it adjusts its behaviour, working out what is required, and continues to successfully pick where required. However, if you had not persevered in giving the dog the same information each time, and instead had given up and moved further forwards to send the dog, or used a different cue to send it, you would not know if the resulting change in behaviour was down to the dog adapting its own behaviour, or down to you adjusting the information you gave to the dog.

You need to give the dog a chance to assimilate the information and then adapt its behaviour. Remaining consistent in your cue will give the dog the best chance to do this and to work out what is required. Too many people, in this instance, when things get tough, are too ready either to give up, or to change their own behaviour, or to quickly over-simplify the task. This is a mistake. The learning will be much easier for the dog if you can remain constant, allowing the dog to adapt or change its own behaviour to get the desired result.

Where shot birds fall is beyond your control.

In her book *Grit: The power of passion and perseverance* (2016), Angela Duckworth describes this persistence to succeed as 'grit', which accurately evokes the determination often needed in training. She maintains that it is not genius that is the driver of success, but a special mixture of passion and perseverance. The ability to stick to your tasks and subsequent goals is crucial here. Persevering will involve repeated deliberate practice and effort.

Whilst it may feel, at times, as if there is no hope with certain issues, it is usually worth continuing to try to resolve the problem. Some people are naturally more resilient than others, and able to persevere where others will want to give up, but it is useful to extend your perseverance if you can. This can be done by maintaining a strong conviction in your training methods, and remaining steadfast in your own abilities as a trainer.

CONTROL THE CONTROLLABLES

Worrying about things that may happen, or that are beyond your control, can be debilitating, and can severely limit progress or achievement. As I was driving to the second day of my first Two-Day Open Retriever Stake with Sybil I was filled with trepidation. We had done some nice work on the first day, and there weren't very many dogs left in for day two, so I should have been feeling positive, but instead I felt anxious and couldn't shake off the concern that we would go straight out 'first dog down' on a runner! Many of us have been there at some point. So I had to have a word with myself, and tried to think about things more clearly and logically.

I came up with the expression 'control the controllables' to help me focus. You can't control how a gun shoots or a bird flies: that is beyond your control. All you can do is ensure that you have done your preparation (through ongoing training), and that you play your part on the day by ensuring that you are alert and mark the birds, and put yourself and the dog in a place where it can mark easily. Your training should also ensure that even if the dog hasn't been able to mark the fall, you can help it to get there quickly and accurately.

You can't change your 'luck' on the day of compe-

Your dog should be steady to shot and fall of game before you compete in field trials.

Preparing your dog for all sorts of different terrain and obstacles is important.

tition, but you can give yourself and your dog every opportunity to shine on the retrieves you are given. Just as in a game of cards, you can't change the hand you are dealt, but you can influence how you play those cards, in the correct order, to your advantage.

Early background work is also critical. You don't want to be worrying about your dog's heelwork in a walked-up situation, its steadiness in a drive, or its deliveries once the bird is picked. All these boxes need to be ticked before you get into competition. I am not saying they will be perfect under ongoing competition conditions, but they need to be solid so that you can compete with confidence and worry about the actual retrieves rather than background things.

Trials often have a way of showing up your weaknesses. If you lack preparation in one area, you will sometimes come unstuck. I remember a championship a few years ago, where a fellow competitor had got through to day two but was worried as she had seen that there were fences on the ground that we had been using. She knew her dog wasn't confident with fences and was worried about it. Sure enough, her first retrieve on day two incorporated a fence and her dog would not go over it. You can't go into a competition just hoping that you won't come across your Achilles heel, or something that you are weak at. You need to train, and then train some more, to ensure the dog is adequately prepared to deal with the eventuality.

Another thing to consider – or rather, not consider – is your fellow competitors. It doesn't matter who they are or what they do. You have no control over that either. If they do poor work, it won't mean that you will win if you do poor work yourself. A wise mentor told me years ago that it's actually 'you against the bird, not you against "him"'. You are judged and graded on the work your dog does. Concentrating on trying to keep consistently 'clean' in this work is more productive than worrying about being better (or worse) than somebody else.

The following are take-away tips to help you maintain control in competition:

- Prepare, prepare, prepare (prior to competing).
- Focus on playing your part on the day: 'control the controllables'.
- Forget your fellow competitors – you can't influence what they do – just enjoy their company.
- Keep yourself, and your dog, well hydrated.

2 BAD BEHAVIOUR

Some of the most hilarious and memorable moments I have encountered have been those of canine 'naughtiness'. And most of them relate to just one particular Labrador that I owned, named Maud. I have so many comical tales relating to competitions that it is hard to know where to start. Maud was the most talented game finder and hunting dog, and was superb at taking runners, but not always the best at working in partnership with me. If I were to describe Maud it would be to say that she was 'consistently inconsistent' in that she was always able to find new ways to surprise or disappoint me: a lovely 'find' on a woodcock closely followed by spitting it out to carry on hunting; tracking a runner and then refusing to recall; and going AWOL in the woods for hours on end are just some of her documented exploits.

In the shooting field a little inconsistency or quirkiness can sometimes be tolerated, and does provide for some amusing anecdotes, but in the competitive world of field trials, when you have often driven hundreds of miles just to reach the venue for the event, you cannot have a dog that repeatedly lets you down.

WHAT IS NAUGHTINESS?

When considering the question of naughtiness in dogs, a useful analogy is to think of the definition of a weed in your garden. The dictionary says this is 'a plant considered undesirable in a particular situation': that is, a plant in the wrong place. In the garden a weed is unwanted, but in a wild flower meadow it is totally acceptable. This definition could also be applied to so-called naughty behaviour in dogs. These animals are just exhibiting behaviour that is inappropriate for their particular setting – not what we want from them at the time.

If dogs are not proactively trying to annoy us, plotting our downfall, or making us pay for some earlier indiscretions, then why do they behave in this way? Often we will hear handlers say '...but he knows what to do. He's just being naughty or stubborn.' But can we really conceive of a dog's actions in these terms? Are dogs capable of acts of deliberate naughtiness, or is this a human concept? In the case of the dog that 'knows this', it is likely to be that he knows a particular behaviour in a particular environment. It

Beautiful flowers or weeds?

is one thing performing a task or behaviour at home, with low distraction levels or on familiar ground, and quite another carrying out that same behaviour on new ground with other dogs and handlers. In fact, it isn't the same behaviour at all. It is more often the case that we haven't adequately prepared the dog for the situation that we have put it in. This is not defiant behaviour, but merely a case of not understanding the given cues in a particular instance.

Undesired behaviour may also be a result of the dog's motivation not being strong enough, or the environmental rewards outweighing those offered by the handler. Dogs largely do what works for them. So, if it is more rewarding to sniff a scent-covered tree stump or hunt the thick cover instead of running across bare grass, then this is what the dog will do. This behaviour may not correspond to what you want at the time. Therefore, as a trainer, you need to learn to motivate your dog and help him engage in the correct behaviour that you require when you want it. In this respect, perceived naughtiness is a breakdown in communications with your dog.

You should also rule out any physical or medical reason why your dog may not be acting as you would desire. Gundogs, and Labradors most particularly, seem to be very stoic when it comes to dealing with pain, and they will bear a lot of discomfort without really showing how much pain they are in. In this respect, it is often difficult to prove that pain is a cause of adverse behaviour. For example, a dog that is reluctant to jump may have issues with its elbows or other orthopaedic conditions, or it may not have been taught the correct technique to jump. It may be suffering pain when it jumps, or it may have a fear of previous pain caused by jumping.

Scientists Mills *et al* (2020) acknowledge the role of pain in problem behaviour but say that because it is not generally reported, it is difficult to understand how widespread it is as an issue. Their research concludes that pain can be a causal factor in between 28 and 82 per cent of cases, and they suggest that it is better for veterinarians to treat suspected pain first, rather than consider its significance only when

Check that there is no physical cause, such as lameness, for a dog's undesired behaviour.

the animal does not respond to behaviour therapy. Likewise, if a dog is urinating a lot during its work, this might have a medical cause, such as a urinary tract infection or issue, or it might be due to psychological or emotional reasons, such as submissive urination whereby the dog is anxious or frightened. You should always seek veterinary advice first to rule out any underlying medical issues.

Stress

One of the leading causes of behaviour that might be deemed as naughty is often stress or pressure felt by the dog. This can be manifested in 'displacement behaviour', if the dog becomes confused or distressed, in the form of frantically running around hunting or ground-sniffing, or stopping to mark or urinate. These behaviours are likely to make the handler even more annoyed, adding to the pressure on the dog, and so the downward spiral continues: the behaviour deteriorates further, and the handler becomes even angrier and more unreliable.

I remember judging a novice field trial some years ago, when one competitor's young dog had been sent on a blind retrieve. It had taken several commands just to get the dog to the area of the fall, and the handler then proceeded to stop, cast and hunt the dog multiple times, with the dog being unable to locate the bird. The dog became more and more unsure of what it was being asked to do. It wasn't used to being repeatedly handled in a competitive environment, and gradually as its confidence diminished, its responsiveness deteriorated. Eventually it just stopped and urinated. The sending judge then asked the handler to call the dog in. Urinating in itself is not naughty behaviour – indeed, it is obviously a vital bodily function, but doing so in this environment is not desirable as it demonstrates an unbusiness-like approach to the job in hand. This poor dog had simply run out of ideas in the given situation, and its

PIP: THE ANXIOUS DOG

Tanya took on Labrador Pip at twenty months old, as she had become too much of a problem for her original owner, who could not cope with her any more. The first year and a half of Pip's life had been spent being told off and punished for being naughty. This naughtiness was most often running off and not wanting to come back.

During the first seven months with Tanya, Pip would run off repeatedly. When she came back, just as she got close, she would run off again. This pattern was the same whether it was on a recall or a retrieve. She would only come into the vicinity of Tanya and then make off again. It appeared as if she were playing a game, which made things very frustrating.

On several occasions it took Tanya over an hour to get Pip back, and even then she was unable to put a lead on her, as she would not come within arm's reach when a lead was in sight. Eventually Tanya resorted to walking away from her and letting Pip follow. Only when her back was turned and she was a distance away would Pip choose to follow her. If Tanya turned back towards her, she would run off again.

Tanya got very frustrated with this process because it looked as if Pip was just being naughty. But it was only when she started some more methodical training, using a clicker in some instances so that Pip could work out what was required, that she realised how quickly Pip was able to learn and how calm she could be when she understood what was required of her. Very soon Tanya understood that the dog was comfortable with patterns of behaviour she understood, but if a new pattern were introduced then she would still exhibit what looked like naughty behaviour, but which was in fact stress.

In this case, the bad behaviours were likely to have been caused by the punishment she received from her previous owner when she did eventually return. This treatment had created anxiety and fear in her about coming back, with the knowledge that the consequences wouldn't be good, and that it would be more pleasant to stay away and enjoy the continued reward of hunting instead.

Early on, Pip played 'keep away' as she had become anxious to return to her previous owner.

Some dogs will 'freeze' if they become stressed.

apparent stress was manifested in the displacement behaviour of urinating.

Dogs behave differently under pressure, much like their human counterparts. We can categorise their behaviour into either positive or negative stress types. Positive stressers tend to speed up their activities, moving around faster and becoming more erratic, confused or busy, whereas negative stressers may often shut down completely, 'freezing' and being unable to move. Our human reaction is often to get cross with the positive stressers, as their behaviour appears naughty and infuriating, and to feel frustrated but sorry for the negative stressers.

Whereas common triggers for stress in wild dogs include lack of food, competition for a mating partner or finding shelter, for our domestic working companions their stress is more likely to come about from being asked to do tasks that they cannot understand or carry out. In addition, it is worth considering that it is not always the actual stressor itself that can cause anxiety. Whilst threat can include physical danger, it can also include just the thought or worry about it too, and thus trigger the same response. In this respect, the fear felt about a snake is the same as actually seeing a snake. When the brain's hypothalamus receives a signal that a threat exists, a chemical chain of reactions releases adrenalin into the bloodstream causing an increased heartbeat, higher blood pressure and heightened senses. The dog can actually end up thinking itself into a state of stress.

It is easy, and rather lazy, to characterise a dog's behaviour as stubborn or wilful. You will often hear handlers say their dog is 'blowing them off', as it chooses to do something else instead of what they require, or 'He's taking the Mickey. He knows what I want!' When you call a dog to you and it doesn't come, it's easy to say 'it won't come' – but instead try looking at why the dog can't come. It may have heard the recall cue but is prevented from coming because the reward it is receiving for its current behaviour is too great. It may be afraid of some sort of conflict, or it may be feeling pain or fatigue. Or it may just be the case that the dog hasn't learnt that behaviour here. In this respect, you will need to look at the environment and all the background conditions that are preventing the behaviour you require.

THE EMOTIONS OF DOGS

French philosopher René Descartes suggested that animals such as dogs were simply programmable machines without consciousness or emotions. However, most modern-day dog owners like to believe that canine emotions are similar to our own. Kujala (2017) agrees that dogs do...

> ...attend to social cues, they respond appropriately to the valence of human and dog facial expressions and vocalisations of emotion, and their limbic reward regions respond to the odor [sic] of their caretakers. They behave differently according to the emotional situation, show emotionally driven expectations, have affective disorders, and exhibit some subcomponents of empathy.

We also know that dogs are avid readers of our body language and facial expressions, able to pick up on subtle nuances and respond accordingly. Kujala adds: 'The canine brain includes a relatively large prefrontal cortex, and like primates, dogs have a brain area specialised for face perception. Dogs have many degrees of emotion, but the full extent of dog emotions remains unknown.'

However, an article by Stanley Coren (2013) maintains that the emotions of dogs are similar to those experienced by a two-year-old child. He says that dogs experience hormonal and chemical changes in the same way as humans, and have the oxytocin hormone that is responsible for feeling love and affection. Coren says that although dogs have similar neurology to humans, they do not have the same emotional range, and he goes on to illustrate that human babies are born with an emotion known as 'excitement' and in later months they develop additional emotions such as fear, disgust and anger. Joy appears to come at around the age of six months, followed by shyness and suspicion, with love not fully developing until the age of about nine to ten months. Finally, the more complex social emotions, such as pride, guilt, shame or contempt, do not come until the child reaches the age of around three to four years.

But Coren says that dogs move through their emotional developmental stages more quickly and will have their full range of emotions (including joy, fear, anger, disgust and love) by the time they reach about six months of age. However, he maintains that they never reach the full range of more complex

Not guilty – the dog understands that the owner is displaying signs of anger.

emotions such as pride, shame or guilt. Some owners are convinced that, when they return home to find their dog has destroyed its bed in their absence, their dog shows guilt or remorse for its naughty behaviour; however, it is more likely that the dog is offering an appeasement posture in deference to their owner's body language or shouting. The dog is incapable of showing guilt, but may feel fear in the face of negative consequences for its actions. It senses that the owner is angry or stressed.

In *The Mind-Gut Connection*, Mayer (2016) reminds us that the physical anatomy of the dog's brain is significantly different in that although dogs do have an anterior insula, which gives humans the ability to feel self-awareness, this, in conjunction with the frontal aspects of their brain, is rudimentary. He posits that: 'Internally generated sensations, including those from the gut, are integrated in the base of their brains and in subcortical emotional centres, rather than in the frontal insular': this makes them emotional, but not with any great degree of self-awareness.

LEFT-PAWED DOGS

Research into lateralisation is also useful in informing our understanding of both behaviour and emotions in dogs. Like humans, dogs usually have a paw preference, and like us they are more likely to be right-handed than left. Also left-handed dogs are more likely to be both male and younger. Whereas, according to Papadatou-Pastou *et al* (2020), around 10 per cent of humans are left-handed, a recent study by Laverack *et al* (2021) determined that of the 74 per cent of dogs exhibiting a paw preference, 58 per cent were right-handed and 42 per cent were left-handed. However, the dogs were tested doing a task of retrieving food from inside a plastic tube, which is a very specific task. From this study, we can surmise that left-handedness is more common in dogs than it is in humans, and that it is affected by both gender and age, with female dogs more likely to be right-handed. This is similar to humans, in that men are more likely to be left-handed (Rife 1940).

Whereas only around 1 per cent of humans are ambidextrous, this percentage is much higher in dogs, at around a quarter of the population. Cultural pressure in humans may account for some of this contrast. Where this difference in lateralisation gets interesting is in the studies done on its effect on canine behaviour. The strength of laterality as well as the direction were both found to have a profound effect on behaviour, with Batt *et al* (2009) noting that dogs with stronger paw preferences were likely to be bolder and more confident, and those with weak paw preferences were likely to be more cautious. Strongly paw-preferenced dogs were also less prone to anxiety and over-arousal, and more playful in new environments, exhibiting calmer reactions to novel stimuli or unknown people.

In another study by Batt *et al* (2008), researchers found that right-pawed dogs (which use the left side of the brain) were easier to train, calmer, and could handle problems more readily, making them more likely to succeed in guide-dog training. They found that left-pawed dogs were more prone to aggressive or fearful behaviour, and had stronger flight or fight reactions. Later research carried out by Barnard *et al* (2018) went further in demonstrating that paw preference could be used as a predictive indicator of the ability to cope with stress (which was measured through cortisol levels as well as observation). They found that the dogs showing left-paw preference (scored through a food retrieval task) were more likely to exhibit stress behaviours such as a low, crouching posture, moving up and down between sitting, lying down and standing, and vocalisation. Their paper concluded that:

> Overall, it appears that a left motor bias may be linked to a more negative affective state, a more reactive coping style, and a more challenging adaptation to novel environments. Assessing paw preference may become a useful tool in detecting different coping strategies in dogs entering a kennel and in reducing stress in target individuals at higher welfare risk.

There are two tests that are commonly used to determine paw preference: the food retrieval test (Marshall-Pescini *et al*, 2013) and the first stepping test (Tomkins *et al*, 2010). Paw preference can be task specific, so it is worth trying both tests and noting the results. The food retrieval test will show up ambilateral dogs, as these will use both paws equally and will sometimes stabilise the toy with both paws, whereas in the stepping test the dog will only be able to choose to step forwards with either one leg or the other. In this respect, the first stepping test is a more consistent indicator of motor bias.

Dog lying down holding a kong with its paw (the kong test).

Food retrieval test
1. Fill a hollow, conical-shaped toy with soft dog food and freeze this prior to testing.
2. With your dog lying down, show it the toy and allow it to sniff it.
3. Place the toy centrally in front of the dog.
4. Record which paw (right or left) the dog uses to hold or stabilise the toy to lick it. If both paws are used equally, record this too.
5. Remove the toy from the dog and repeat the exercise up to 25 times.

First step test
You will need a helper to monitor and record results, or you can use a video camera set up on a tripod.
1. Stand with your dog at heel, at the top of a step. The dog should also be in a standing position.
2. Step down and record with which leg the dog took its first step.
3. Repeat the exercise up to 25 times.

Alternatively, you can leave the dog standing at the top of the step alone, and call it down towards you. This will remove any bias of having the dog at heel on your left, or being influenced by the leg that you lead with.

First step test: (top) Brae proved to be consistently right-legged, while (below) Twig had a greater preference for the left leg.

So, when considering your own dog's undesirable behaviour, it might be worth determining its paw bias to see if it is more likely to be affected by stressful situations. There are a few complicating variables, in that puppies and young dogs show more right-paw bias, which may change as the dog matures, and, as noted above, female dogs are predominantly right-pawed, whereas males are more prone to left-paw bias.

Paw preference, as well as having potential emotional consequences, will also sometimes physically affect the gundog in its work when it comes to handling. For example, a dog that has stopped remotely facing its owner and is given a 'back' command may consistently favour turning on a particular shoulder to go back, rather than going back the way it is directed by the handler. This is not neces-

Tail wagging to the right – this dog is happy and relaxed.

sarily naughtiness or defiance, but simply a strong muscle memory, or doing what is more comfortable physically for the dog.

Laterality in dogs also goes beyond just paw preference, and can be seen in how dogs relate to positive and negative stimuli, in terms of moving towards this source. When the brain processes positive experiences associated with familiarity, or emotions such as affection, happiness and excitement, the left hemisphere is activated. Conversely, the right hemisphere is used when it processes fear, sadness or novel experiences. Studying humans, Ahern and Schwartz (1979) found that when people were asked questions provoking positive emotions they looked to their right (demonstrating left brain involvement), and conversely when they answered questions that evoked negative emotions they looked to their left, showing right brain hemisphere involvement.

Through an understanding of lateralisation, you have the potential to improve the quality of life for your dog in stressful situations, helping it to behave appropriately, and in turn, making your training more effective. For example, you can reduce potential stress by approaching dogs from their right side in veterinary examinations or during greetings. And by paying attention to the way in which dogs turn, we are also able to see how they are reacting emotionally to various stimuli (Siniscalchi *et al*, 2010). In addition, the asymmetry in dogs' tail wags is useful to ascertain their overall emotional state – as a rule, wagging to the right is a happy, positive and relaxed sign, whereas wagging to the left indicates concern and negative emotions.

Therefore, there are several factors (both emotional and physical) that you need to consider when trying to understand your dog's so-called bad behaviour.

3 REHOMING

Rehoming, or 'moving on' a gundog can be an emotive subject. When people purchase a dog to be a pet or companion it is usually for life, and they accept and love it with all its faults and foibles. Gradually the dog fits into family life, and if necessary, adaptations and compromises are made on both sides. Pet owners are unlikely to rehome their dog unless there is a significant change in family circumstances, such as illness or job loss.

Conversely, it is not unusual for professional gundog trainers to move dogs on that they feel are not fit for the purpose for which they were intended. The role of a sporting dog that is bought or bred to do a specific job is very different to that of a pet dog. Whilst these dogs are also predominantly loved and loyal pets they are also regarded variously as athletes, 'tools of the job' and as top-level competitors.

People who work their dogs usually have a very good knowledge of the traits and requirements of the breed they have chosen. In most cases you will have bought the appropriate type of gundog for the work that you want it to do – for example, a Labrador with a thick coat for wildfowling, a pointing breed for work on the grouse moor, or a Springer spaniel to quest through cover on a rough shoot.

You will also have put a great deal of consideration into choosing the right dog for your needs within your chosen breed. It is likely that you have researched pedigrees thoroughly, as well as health tests and the working achievements of both parents, and have selected what you think will provide you with the dog with the right temperament. Then you will have spent weeks, months, or even years training your young dog. However, despite all of this groundwork, you may find that the dog you have isn't working out in line with your expectations. This might be for a number of reasons, including faults that would preclude the dog from the shooting field, such as having a hard mouth or being gun-shy, through other undesirable traits, such as making noise or unsteadiness, down to a simple clash of personalities.

As with any working partnership, the dog and trainer should both complement and like each other. You will be asking a lot of your dog as you train it, so building a good bond and trust is paramount. You will need to protect and nurture this. Sometimes, after an honest appraisal, it takes courage to admit that the

The relationship with your dog is of primary importance.

partnership isn't working, for whatever reason. If this is the case, you will need to look at ways to rectify this, or should consider parting company as the best option for both parties.

Relationship is one of the hardest things to change. You can work on conditioning different behaviours and responses to cues, and improving reliability in this respect, but the one thing that transcends all this is the rapport that you have with your dog. Gundog training is often more of a gut feeling than a scientific equation of triggering responses. How true, then, the expression 'one man's meat is another man's poison'. We all like different things, and the type of trainer that you are will mean that a certain type or temperament of dog may suit you better than others. For example, some people look for a dog with a calm nature that readily takes input from its handler, whereas others demand something with more fire in its belly and a much more outgoing nature.

If you are part-way through your training journey with your dog and realise that the relationship is not working for either party, you will need to assess whether it is worth persevering: should you invest more time and money into training this dog, with the

If you have a strong bond with your dog, you will overcome the challenges ahead.

hope that progress can be made, or should you part company and give both yourself and the dog a fresh start?

When I have seen clients facing extreme struggles, with complicated training challenges, and they ask me whether their issues can be solved, my answer is always the same: 'Do you like the dog?' If you have a great relationship with your dog and you really love it, you will work hard to find a solution. You will want to overcome the difficulties together, or accept what you have got. But if you aren't fully invested in the dog, then you will find it very tough indeed.

Whilst you may not like the young dog you have got, it is also important to remember that the dog may not like you, and therefore may not be motivated to work with you. You can adjust your training to suit the type of dog you have, but it is very hard to change your own nature. In this case it is often better to find a different job or a different owner for this dog.

SUITABLE FIT

When training a dog for field trials in particular, you will need to consider whether it is suitable to do the work you are requiring of it, and if not, whether it is ethical to continue to push it into a role that it is not capable of fulfilling. In every well-bred litter there are likely to be some dogs that will meet the standards required for competing, and others that will not. The same goes for humans. For example, when I was young, I enjoyed gymnastics. I competed at an amateur school level, but was never going to reach a more advanced stage as I struggled to do the box splits. Despite lots of practice, I wasn't physically cut out for the role. I made a passable gymnast at County level, but I was never going to progress beyond that. Needless to say, it was not a path that I or my parents continued to pursue for myself.

Forcing a dog to do something that it is not mentally or physically capable of doing isn't ethical, and it is up to us as trainers to understand and work with the limitations of our dogs, or to accept when it isn't the right dog for the job. Detractors from field trials are

VERA: YOU GET WHAT YOU WANT, BUT NOT WHAT YOU NEED!

Vera was lively and distracted from the outset.

On paper, Vera had it all. She was out of the litter sister to one of the best bitches that I have ever owned, which was put to a dog with equally strong credentials. I felt the pairing would give me some outstanding qualities, including plenty of drive, determination and excellent hunting abilities.

There were only two bitches in the litter, which meant that choosing one should have been more straightforward. This was one of the few litters that I had temperament tested to see what traits were coming through, using the American Avidog Puppy Evaluation Testing (APET) system. I hoped that this would be useful in informing my decision-making process.

Going through all the evaluations, both Vera and the other bitch scored highly for retrieve, play and food motivation. They were extremely biddable, had high energy levels, moderate environmental focus, learned quickly, were not easily stressed, and readily engaged with people. There was nothing much between them, and so I picked the black one for a change.

Within days of her being home, I already had a sense of Vera. She was a lively puppy but she didn't bond readily with me. Her gaze was always elsewhere. Right from the outset, getting a reliable recall was something that I struggled with, and this was a pattern that was set to continue. If Vera was anywhere, she was elsewhere. She was very distracted, with one of the highest environmental focuses I have seen, and had very little regard for me as her handler or partner; however, I persisted with her training.

Nothing came easily in terms of schooling.

Because of her poor recall, we suffered all sorts of issues with retrieving (swapping, hunting on, detouring). She was also very hard to get steady, and had a lot of trouble with delivery. However, we worked through all these issues and made good progress, eventually getting to where I expected to be. But it was a struggle, and I found her extremely frustrating to train as she was inconsistent and distracted. Nevertheless some of her work was also very good. She hunted stylishly, and had strong drive on marked retrieves. She definitely had the ability, and I was absolutely sure that she would 'make the grade' as far as work was concerned.

What was completely lacking, though, was any sort of rapport between us. Because she was so frustrating to train, I didn't look forward to, or enjoy, taking her out, and would often avoid it – and this was no way to start a lifelong partnership of work. Still I kept going with her. At one year old she passed all her health tests with flying colours – but that didn't make me love her any more. And in the following months, I finally decided that the best option for both of us would be to part company.

Although it was a difficult decision, the sense of relief I felt was also palpable. I had no doubt that this very talented young dog had a bright future ahead of her, but just not with me. She had all the ability to reach the highest level, but I didn't want to go there with her – so finding her a new, loving home was the right thing to do for both of our sakes.

My time was not wasted with Vera, and I learned a lot from the experience. Not only did I refresh my training skills on some core issues (which we will look at in Part II), but I reminded myself that 'bond' really is everything. I would happily sacrifice a piece of that talent for more of a connection. You can't train that.

quick to criticise competition trainers for 'getting rid of' or even 'disposing of' dogs that don't make the grade. However, nothing could be further from the truth. Using their skill and experience they have realised that some dogs will be happier elsewhere fulfilling a different role.

World-renowned horse trainer Monty Roberts very powerfully summed up the importance of the relationship between the trainer (rider) and the animal in his book *The Horses in my Life* (2004), when he wrote about a horse called Julia's Doll. He said that the greatest lesson this horse taught him was that...

> *...a good trainer needs to bury his ego and respect the wishes of his equine student. Find the thing they want to do most and help them to do it, even if it doesn't involve you personally. A selfish attitude in training horses will eventually come back to haunt you, the same as it will in human relationships.*

The same philosophy can equally be applied to training gundogs.

BUYING A PART-TRAINED DOG

The other side of the rehoming scenario is taking on a dog from elsewhere. This is not without its challenges, not least because, in many cases, you won't know what has happened in the dog's past to inform his current behaviour. In this respect, many rehomed dogs may come with 'baggage' due to their uncertain background.

It takes time for a dog to settle into its new environment and to establish trust. It is as much you learning about the dog as it is him learning about you, and how he should behave in his new home. You can't rush this process and force the dog to like you. It is likely that you will face additional challenges due to you not being able to build that bond from scratch yourself, or from you not understanding the dog's full history.

If the dog you are taking on comes from a professional trainer, it is likely to be well trained already, but may not be a good fit for what they required. This could be a matter of clashing personalities, either with the trainer or with other dogs in the kennel. Or it could be that the dog has a fault that would preclude

Working in the beating line is ideal for a spaniel that won't retrieve.

HOLLY: THE PRELOVED RETRIEVER (by Jill G)

Christmas 2012 was a sad one, as I had lost my seven-year-old working golden retriever due to several health issues. She was an important part of my picking-up team, and now there was a gaping hole. I was faced with either buying a puppy, which was not really what I wanted, or trying to find something 'part-trained'. Whilst making

Holly proved her capability in the field, after a difficult start.

enquiries, I happened across a Free Ads advertisement that read: 'Three-year-old working-type golden retriever bitch; child's allergy forces sale.' As a golden retriever owner and trainer, with 25 years' experience, it went totally against the grain to contemplate buying a dog in this way, but after a conversation with the owner I thought it was worth investigating. I made the long journey to meet the shy but beautiful dog that growled nervously at me at first. We went on a walk, and although she showed no interest in the dummies I had brought with me to assess her interest in retrieving, she was keen to fetch a tennis ball and hunted enthusiastically.

A week later, I collected Holly. Although she was anxious when I first got home, it didn't take her long to establish a rapport with my own dogs and start playing with them. She had obviously missed exercise and contact with other dogs. The next day I walked Holly to my local vet for a check-up. She dragged me along, and her heelwork was extremely poor.

Once she had settled in, I began introducing some basic training, treating her as if she were a puppy, and she loved the challenge of doing something new. To get over her initial lack of interest in dummies, I let her run in, making retrieving a lot of fun, and we played hunting games in the long grass. Soon she was picking canvas with enthusiasm. With heelwork I had to go back to the start and work on rewarding literally one step at a time when she stayed in the desired position.

Holly relished the mental stimulation and improved rapidly. Over the summer I was able to include her on some group training sessions, and in September, I took the plunge and entered her in a walked-up novice retriever working test. It was nerve-racking, bearing in mind how bad her heelwork had been six months previously, and the fact that she still had limited handling ability. However, she proved to be incredible at marking and came away with a certificate of merit.

The next challenge was introducing her to cold game, and she took to that readily. In the autumn, I took her to a couple of walked-up rough shoot days, where she just had one or two retrieves under live shot. She was so well behaved that a couple of weeks later I was able to take her picking up for the first time. It was as if she had been doing the job all her life: she was quiet, steady, and most importantly, was able to find game. She completed the whole season, and in a very short space of time had become totally integrated into my team, and worth her weight in gold.

After the season I continued to work hard on Holly's training, and over the next four years she far exceeded my expectations by winning numerous working test awards and proving to be an exceptional game finder in the field, the best I'd had in a long time.

I still marvel at the chain of events that brought Holly to me. I took a chance, even a risk, on buying her, but she gave me far more than I could ever have imagined. Would I do it again? Probably not – I could never be that lucky again!

I had a message from one of the owners of a puppy that I had bred, saying that he had decided to part company with her, because he had not really taken to her and thought she had a timid nature. Did I know of anyone looking for a young dog from my breeding? Without hesitation I said I would like the opportunity to buy her back if possible. I drove to meet her owner, who gave me her papers and some of her current food, and told me her name was 'Twig'. He said she was fast, came back when you called her, and that her heelwork was okay. The irony of the situation was clear to me in that, just three months before, I had myself rehomed Vera, also because she wasn't a good match for me – and this bitch had the same sire. But I was curious to see what Twig was like.

Twig very quickly found her way into my affections!

Once home, she settled in to family life at Stauntonvale very quickly. We had her in the house with us for the first few days, and only then moved her to the kennel. Thankfully she was clean and got on well with the other dogs. She had had some rudimentary training, but her heelwork was not acceptable for competition standard, and she was completely unsteady to a thrown dummy. She was also a ball of nervous energy and excitement.

We started work on building a bond and trust, and then the foundation work began on her training. I helped her establish an understanding of where I wanted her heel position to be, by using a clicker to mark this, and she was very quick to pick things up. In Part II you will see how I worked on steadiness, lining out to blind retrieves and some of the other issues.

In the first few days after Twig's arrival, I didn't know where this journey would take us, but I did know that we both liked each other, and that was a good start. However, after several

it from competition. However, this doesn't mean that the dog would not be suitable for working in the field. For example, a spaniel that is great at hunting but doesn't retrieve will not be suitable for field trials, but would be a valuable addition to the beating line at a shoot. Likewise, a Labrador that lacks pace and style won't progress to the highest ranks in competition, but would be ideal as a peg dog or as part of a picking-up team.

However, some 'second-hand' dogs will suffer from mistakes having been made, or from gaps in their education. Therefore in some cases you will need a degree of flexibility in how you approach the training of a rehomed dog. You will also need to be realistic in your expectations.

When seeking out a part- or fully trained gundog to join your team, it is very much a case of caveat emptor. Ensure that you research the pedigree, background and circumstances surrounding the dog that is being offered for sale or for rehoming before weeks of concerted work, I began to see some of the issues that may have frustrated her previous owner, and any thoughts of a 'quick fix' began to vanish as I realised that a few areas were going to take a lot of work. She had a lot of belief in her own ability, and was not so willing to take on board help or input from me.

Some of the environmental factors that I had observed about Vera were very noticeable with Twig too, namely that she was very distracted by things going on around her (other dogs, other retrieves, people), and this meant that she found it very hard to focus on what I wanted her to do. The difference, though, was that we developed a bond for each other almost instantly, so I knew that I would be able to work through some of these issues over time and with patience.

Twig was 'behind' in her abilities, and very distracted in her work.

you make any commitment. The terms 'part-trained' and 'fully trained' mean different things to different people. So ensure that you have a full understanding of what level of training has been put into the dog, and ask for a demonstration on neutral ground, with retrieves set up by yourself, so that you can assess its real potential. Both parties should also agree to a trial period to ensure that the new home is a good fit.

Even if the dog you have bought, or brought in, has been trained, you will still have to do some

back-tracking to ensure that it is working with you, and understands the subtle differences of the new partnership with you, as opposed to its previous owner or handler. In some cases, for certain skills, it may be a case of 'starting from scratch', although this is not really possible as the dog will already have a history of behaviour. It isn't the blank canvas that a baby puppy represents.

Undoing ingrained behaviour patterns and trying to retro-fit training to a more mature dog is not a straightforward task, and will require a degree of patience, understanding and creativity. You will need to take more time to observe the dog and how it is relating to both you and its work. Where you see incongruences, try to isolate these and develop a methodical plan to work on each of these areas.

Two months after signing the contract for *Gundog SOS*, I was myself given the opportunity to take on a young dog that needed to be rehomed. The timing was uncanny, as we would need to work through a lot of issues together.

When taking on an older dog, as well as undoing some undesirable habits, and not having a solid known foundation of basic training, further difficulties may arise due to your own expectations and those of other people. For example, if you have a younger puppy that is more reliable and advanced in its training, despite being several months or even years younger, it is difficult not to compare this dog, or feel pressurised and frustrated by the newcomer being somewhat 'behind' in its training. It will feel as if there is a huge list of skills that need to be taught and understood by the newcomer dog just to get it 'up to speed'.

It can be hard to put aside these feelings of expectation, especially when other people ask how old your dog is. But you will need to deal with this and try to devise a methodical training plan that incorporates small wins to keep you on track for eventual success, all be that a lot further down the line. Trying to do too much, too quickly to 'catch up' will only end in frustration, as that flawed plan inevitably doesn't work out.

4 FINDING A WAY FORWARDS

When you reach an impasse with a difficult dog, or you have ongoing issues that you feel you are not able to resolve, it can be very hard to find the will to continue. It feels so frustrating to invest your time and energy into something where you are not making any visible progress or improvement: it feels as if it isn't worth the effort that you are putting in. But there are very few paths in life that are completely free of setbacks or potholes along the way.

However, these struggles are often useful to build resilience, and indeed, scientists have proved that there is much truth in Friedrich Nietzche's phrase 'what doesn't kill you makes you stronger'. Researchers at the Kellogg School of Management, Northwestern University, USA have established a causal relationship between failure and future success. They assessed the relationship between professional failure and success for young scientists, and found that those who had early knockbacks had greater long-term success after trying again. The study (Wang *et al*, 2019) concluded that 'setbacks are an integral part of a scientific career', and Wang reminds us that 'while we have been relatively successful in pinpointing the benefits of success, we have failed to understand the impact of failure.' He points out that there is value in failure, and that this research is being expanded into other fields.

DEALING WITH FAILURE AND FEAR

Used intelligently, then, failure can be a vital component along the path to success. When you have failures, it is important to learn from them and then try

It is better to keep a dog on the lead to prevent the reward of a chase.

to modify your behaviour so that the same conditions don't occur again, and you don't end up repeating them. For example, on a walk if your dog is running ahead and it puts up a rabbit and bolts after it, and you blow your recall whistle and it doesn't return, there are several learning points that can be taken on board to ensure the situation isn't repeated, risking another failure. You could keep a closer eye on the dog and not let it range too far away so that your connection with it is broken; you could keep the dog on the lead; and you could take care not to blow your recall whistle in a situation where you know there is no chance the dog is in a position to respond to it. In this respect, failure is temporary and has led to learning and problem solving. Try not to focus on what has happened, but rather on how you responded to it. This will help you to move forwards.

When you are defeated by something, it can feel that your effort was wasted – but you still have the goal that you were working towards. So you have to pick up the pieces and re-order them so that they bring you back on track. Rather than always focusing on the losses, try to look also at the parts of the journey that bring you joy and satisfaction. For example, you might be battling to achieve a consistent outrun with a dog on blinds, but remember how good your dog is at hunting, and try to incorporate moments in your training where you continue to celebrate these triumphs.

Inevitably in the course of gundog training you will feel as if it is one step forwards and two steps back, but Bruce Lee once likened this to cracking the combination of a safe: turning the knob once rarely unlocked the safe, but you need to advance and retreat in carefully orchestrated combinations, and this will eventually unlock the safe to reveal the treasure. Knowing when to go forwards, when to go back, and when to change tack forms the art of gundog training.

Not achieving what you set out to do, or the dog not operating as you expected, is usually because the dog doesn't understand the task in its current

The dog may show displacement behaviours such as urinating or eating grass.

environment, or it is beyond its current level of training. If this is repeated it can lead to a negative state in which the dog moves into displacement behaviour such as ground sniffing, lying down, running off or eating grass. In these cases, it is not that the dog is being distracted by the environment, which is the interpretation many trainers make in this situation, but rather, the dog is distracted by its own negative internal emotions (the sniffing or chewing is just a way of releasing these).

If the dog is failing and is disengaged you need to change the criteria you have set for the exercise (again, simplify), and/or change the motivation or reward for the dog in order to ensure success. When any of these negative aspects creeps in then suspend your training and review what you are doing. It may be appropriate to have a break and start again another day, when you have had time to assess what has happened and have put a plan in place for a more positive outcome next time.

Your own fear can also be a limiting factor, so it is important to understand and recognise this. Fear and worry may be for a variety of reasons, including fear of losing, of embarrassment, of letting people down, of not performing to others' expectations, and of making mistakes. Wanting to avoid all these fears is understandable but it can be debilitating, so it is important to acknowledge fear, but be deliberate in not giving it any power to influence your actions or shrink your ambition. If you allow worry to consume you, then this will become your guiding beacon, and in this respect will become a self-fulfilling prophecy.

THE IMPORTANCE OF TRUST

As we have discussed in Chapter 3, it is important that the dog and trainer should fit each other, and moreover like each other. A good relationship will always be paramount when you are working intensely with a gundog, and you need to protect and nurture that. If the dog doesn't like you and, more importantly, doesn't trust you, he will not be motivated to work with you.

Trust needs to be built up between dog and handler.

believing that someone is good, sincere and honest.

Behavioural scientists Martin and Friedman, in a speech delivered at the IAATE Conference 2013, suggested that when trust is established between humans and animals then animals are more motivated to learn. They state that 'trusting animals use their behaviour to confidently approach, rather than escape, opportunities to interact with people. They not only accept invitations to interact with their trainers, but trusting animals create interaction opportunities for their trainers as well.'

However, the concept of trust is not black and white, in that you either have it or you don't, but seems to be built up in complex layers. A dog may learn to trust you because pleasant things happen around you, but then again that trust can be eroded or spoilt through carelessness. Think about recalling a dog that is running away or free hunting. Normally you reward the dog for coming back to you, so it trusts that coming back is pleasant or enjoyable. Now think of the time that the dog didn't come back promptly and you got annoyed and told it off when it came

Trust is an interesting concept. A dictionary definition of trust is 'the firm belief in the reliability, truth, or ability of someone or something' – for example, 'relationships have to be built on trust'. Other definitions include having confidence in somebody, and

Successfully lining up for a blind retrieve requires trust from the dog.

back. This will have had an adverse effect on how the dog relates to returning to you, and in future it may not trust you as much in this respect.

Martin and Friedman use a bank account analogy to describe the trust relationship. You have to build up significant deposits, which rely on positive interactions to build a 'bank of trust'. They say that withdrawals from this account, through negative interactions such as using punishment, will erode the balance and can build up negatively over time to push the relationship into the red. Therefore it is important that you make many more positive 'deposits' than negative withdrawals.

It is worth reviewing your relationship with your dog and ensuring that your trust bank is full, so that he can weather any short-term losses or difficulties. When it comes to handling and, in particular, working a dog on blind retrieves, you will need the dog to place his trust in you fully, putting his own beliefs to one side temporarily. For example, your dog may have marked a pheasant straight ahead of him, but you need to send him at a tight angle for another bird, which he hasn't seen, that is running into a hedge. He should be able to take on your direction, effectively putting all his eggs in your basket, ignoring what he has seen and trusting that he will find a retrieve where you are directing him. Equally, when he is working on a retrieve that you have seen come down and that you feel you have marked accurately, and he starts to pull away out of the area, you will need to trust his natural instincts and judgement because his nose will become his primary detection sense over your eyes at this point. Trust works both ways in this respect.

IMPROVING LEARNING

There is an art to learning, or rather a process, and an understanding of some of the rules will help both you and your dog to learn more efficiently. There are a few techniques that you can use to aid learning and to support your dog in processing new information in a timely manner; these are described in the following sections.

Work on individual elements such as hunting separately.

Count Repetitions, not Time

How often have you been asked 'how many times a week do you train?' or 'how many hours training have you done?'? Time is often used as a yardstick to measure training input. However, it is not really the best nor the most appropriate measure. Three hours standing in a field with a group of friends, periodically sending your dog up the side of a hill to collect a retrieve, is not necessarily focused activity. Instead you might be better off going out alone with your dog for ten minutes and performing repetitions of a core skill that needs work, such as repetition of a 'back' command under certain conditions.

Engaging in useful repetitions will help wire connections in the dog's brain. This power of repetition is used by musicians, sports competitors and athletes as they drill their skills to hone performance. It is also far more measurable in that you know whether you have completed the task, and how many times you have repeated it.

Chunking, then Chaining

We talked about training in bite-sized pieces in Chapter 1. Rather than tackling complex retrieves as a whole, try to break down the exercise into smaller component parts or chunks. Work on each of these individual skills separately. For example, you may have found that when you issue a 'hunt' cue your dog does not hold its ground and stay in the required area, but your outrun and stop whistle have both been perfect. In this instance you can work on improving the hunt chunk in a standalone static exercise. Once this has been improved you can add it back into the sequence.

If you are teaching the dog a new skill or behaviour chain, try to break it down into small chunks. In this way you can work on each part individually before moving on and building the chain. It is much clearer and quicker to work on individual tasks than trying to master the process as a whole. The dog's understanding will be much deeper once he has been given time to work on component parts separately, and he will be able to recall these abilities into different chains more quickly in the future.

Make it a Game

You may have heard trainers say 'try making it more fun', or 'make it into a game', but it might not have seemed appropriate for the serious work that a gundog is asked to do in the field. However, brains like games. Creating a game whereby the dog has to learn the rules of engagement and how it can earn a series of rewards is fun for both dog and handler, and will also go a long way towards improving or maintaining your relationship. Paying rewards leads to the formation of habits and will help crystallise learning.

Allow Time to Refresh

Training is draining, for the dog as well as the handler. If you are using the techniques above, there will be a lot of information flowing into your dog's brain, and this will use considerable mental energy. It is therefore important that you give the dog adequate time to switch off completely and relax without being disturbed.

If the dog is involved in athletic exercises, such as running through difficult terrain, jumping and swimming, then it will become physically tired. But it will also become mentally fatigued because it has to focus or concentrate over a sometimes extended period of time. Also, if you have a dog that is high energy and is highly aroused, it may not be 'switch-

Ensure your dog has time for adequate rest after training or competing.

Working in a group can provide support and encouragement.

ing off' between exercises and will be maintaining itself in a state of anticipation, and this will use up a lot of energy.

Rest is required to improve brain function. The brain will learn best when it is rested and refreshed, so intersperse your chunks of training with adequate periods of rest.

RETAINING MOTIVATION

Keeping motivated with training, particularly in the long, cold winter months, can be quite a struggle. And many gundog trainers find that with hardly any daylight hours to fit round the constraints of working or picking-up days, there is little time for much meaningful training during the winter. But as the days start to lengthen, it is time to start turning your thoughts to kickstarting your motivation to train again. One of these ways is to set some goals. These goals can take two forms, performance goals and process goals, and both are equally valid.

Performance Goals

Preparing for a competition can be a great way of keeping up your motivation and momentum in training. Having something to aim for where you know your skills will be tested will help keep you on track with regular training. With performance goals you put in the work, achieve them, celebrate and move on. These can be very rewarding for the trainer as there is a definite goal or endpoint.

Process Goals

Process goals are not as straightforward. When you first start training a young pup, you may be full of energy and inspiration, and be committed to doing regular small amounts of training. Mini goals, such as teaching a sit for dinner time or walking off-lead at heel, provide regular 'wins' along the way. However, further on in training as your dog gets closer to being ready for a shoot day there seems to be a 'sticky middle'. Progress becomes slow and sometimes hard to measure. This is true for most long-term projects. For example, if you are dieting, making a healthy choice today, picking a green salad rather than chips, is not going to make you look or feel obviously different straightaway. So it is very hard to stick to this sort of process goal until you can see some sort of progress. In the case of dieting, that would be eventual measurable weight loss; with dog training, that may be that your dog stops its repeated running in as a result of your consistency in training.

Many handlers who are going through this difficult middle patch feel that this is a good time to give up and find a less frustrating hobby. However, try to set clear micro goals, and dig deep for the determination and stamina required to keep going and stick to the task.

Get Some Support

In the Introduction we talked about enlisting the help of a professional trainer or mentor to provide objective input and guidance to keep you on the right track. It is also a great support to have like-minded friends to

Prize-winning dogs still have flaws!

train with. Being part of a training group or community will help you stay motivated and refreshed with new ideas. The power of the group will also mean that you can build accountability and help each other.

The other thing that you can do is engineer reinforcement for yourself around those process goals – and that doesn't mean incentivising each training session with a chocolate bar afterwards! Although that may help a little. It means creating some achievable checklists. Break down some of your training elements into component elements to work on individually, and then you can tick them off each time you do them. It's not a difficult thing to do, but it is very satisfying. And seeing a row of ticks on your training notepad makes you realise that you are doing something, and achieving those goals, and those ticks will gradually build up.

A colleague mentioned to me the value of a 'Ta Da' list versus a 'To Do' list too. This means you record the things you have achieved, rather than all the things you still have left to do. This helps to reinforce your efforts in meeting daily and weekly process goals.

Keep it Bite-Sized

Next time you need more motivation, try to break down what needs to be done into smaller and less intimidating goals – take 'baby' steps. Sometimes looking at the big picture and all the phases involved can be daunting, and the single most powerful motivator is small, daily progress. Experiencing setbacks can be very damaging to results. If you can facilitate progress then you can enable better results. Manufacture your own momentum to score a few daily or weekly wins. This is important to do because your confidence is either lifted up or dragged down depending on your ability to make progress. When you make advances there is something at work that psychologists refer to as 'goal gradient', meaning that the closer you get to something, the harder you are willing to work to achieve it.

PROBLEM SOLVING: USING LANGUAGE AND THOUGHT

Show me a gundog and you will be able to show me a 'problem'. As we have discussed earlier, there isn't a flawless gundog out there, although paradoxically we all like to think that we each own the perfect dog. People are sometimes surprised when I point to my kennels and say there are several field trial champions in there but not one of them is perfect and they all have their own issues and weaknesses.

When training a gundog, it is up to us to work with the dog in front of us to improve on any weak areas and to try to build a better all-round hunting companion. But what can you do when you feel the problem you have is insurmountable, or is really getting you down? Sometimes just taking a step back from the situation and trying to view it from an outsider's point of view can really help.

In his book *Chatter: The voice in our head and how to harness it* (2022), Ethan Kross talks about the discussions he had with his colleagues about the relationship between language and distance, and suggests the idea of using your own name to refer to yourself, silently, rather than out loud. This is a good way to control your inner critical voice. For example, imagine yourself as a character in a book and describe your thoughts and actions from a third-party perspective. He also looked at this for resolving conflict and relationship problems. If people could look at themselves as a couple from the outside, looking in, rather than actually 'being' the couple, they could be a lot more objective and reasoned in their thoughts and discussion.

This same perspective can be transferred to the training field, to view what is going on between you and your dog. For example, you have a problem with a young dog's sendaway, and it is really getting you down. You love the dog so you are obviously emotionally involved with its life, and you want to make things better. You are with the dog the whole time, and all you can see when you try to do retrieves is this issue that doesn't seem to be improving and you don't know how to tackle it. You are on the 'inside' and can't see a way out.

Now imagine that this issue is actually happening to a friend of yours. They are distraught. It is upsetting them a lot. Think about what you would say to

Try to view the situation as others might, from the 'outside' looking in.

that friend, and how you could attempt to help them, from the outside looking in. Taking that step back, distancing yourself from the scenario is often enough to clarify thoughts more objectively, and help you plan a way forwards. What advice would you give to that friend? The other strategy to try is to use 'self-talk', where you address yourself using your name. Again, this is a way of distancing yourself from yourself, and addressing this issue as a spectator rather than as a participant. So you might ask yourself: What should Sarah do now?

Mental distance can help you to control anxiety, and to manage your nerves, too. There is research (Tackman et al, 2019) to show that 'I-talk' – the use of the first-person singular pronoun – is reliably linked to negative emotion. That is, talking to yourself, or about yourself, using 'I' or 'me' can make you more likely to drown in self-pity.

Kross's idea of 'distanced self-talk' was to have people use their name as well as the second- or third-person pronoun to create emotional distance. For example, rather than saying 'Why did I send my dog that way?' you could say 'Why did Kevin send his dog that way?'. This distancing is a psychological hack that can provide diverse benefits including overcoming nerves, increasing confidence, improving problem solving, and promoting the realisation that some of the issues we are worrying about are largely inconsequential in the grand scheme of things.

And whilst this technique is very productive concerning results, it is also low effort, and not draining neural resources, which is critical if you are feeling stressed. Those who employ this method are actually able to turn perceived threats into challenges instead, which is a much more positive viewpoint.

Being a coach, I am in a privileged position with clients so I can put myself in this 'distanced view' position fairly frequently, and can 'look in' at the issues that handlers are experiencing. It has certainly helped me to think and advise with much greater clarity and calmness. However, I still have to remind myself to apply this same approach when I am out with my own dogs.

Prepare and Plan

Design your training sessions for what you are trying to achieve. Think about which areas need improvement, and how you can work in a progressive manner to achieve this over time. This may mean dedicating several sessions over a course of weeks or months to get to where you want to be. In many cases, progress can be slow, and you will come across setbacks, but you are working to get an overall picture of improvement.

Set up your sessions so that they incorporate a repetition of success. This will help consolidate learning (and enjoyment for both dog and handler). The majority of your time should be spent teaching rather than testing the dog. And whilst it is great to have goals, try not to be obsessed with the 'end product'. Gundog training is a journey, so revel in the process rather than just the outcome.

Communicate Clearly

Our dogs are a different species, and don't have the wide repertoire of spoken language that we do. They rely a lot on reading body language. Try to use consistent commands at all times, whatever your mood or level of frustration. 'Back', 'BACK' and 'go back' in differing levels or tones of voice are all different commands. It can be helpful to analyse your body language (using video) or record your voice.

The same applies for the use of your whistle. Is it consistent? It should be strong enough to be heard at distance or against the wind, but should not be blown for an extended time. It should be used as a definite command that sounds positive to the dog. Being consistent in all your communications will help the dog understand what you want.

Timing is also critical. Feedback or communication with the dog needs to be precisely at the time that coincides with the behaviour that you want to mark. Use praise to reward what you want to see more of – this might be stylish hunting, a strong outrun, neat heelwork. Poor timing can lead to confusion.

Fit the Training to the Dog

Adapt to the dog in front of you: don't make your dog fit your training plans. Some trainers who have had previous dogs try not to 'make the same mistake with this dog'. But this is a mistake in itself, as no two dogs are truly alike. Making sure this dog is steady because the last one was poor at heel is not a great plan. By all means learn by your previous training mistakes, but don't assume your next dog will be the same.

Equally, all dogs mature at different rates. Some assimilate their lessons quickly and are ready to progress fairly rapidly, whereas others need additional time just to mature or become ready for more teaching input. You have to assess the dog in front of you. Help your dog become the best that he can, but recognise his strengths and weaknesses. Train according to these, helping to strengthen areas where he is weaker. Required core behaviours don't change, but how you achieve them with each dog can be very different.

Strive to Achieve Balance

Often when we are working on one area of training, for example if the dog is weak at blinds, you may start to become overly focused on this aspect. Try to maintain a balance in your work together. Training that enhances one aspect of work can often diminish another. I've often described gundog training to students as being like a pair of control pants! They enhance one area of your body, but then all the stuff that has been squeezed from one area, suddenly pops back out in another! It's an ongoing process of management.

Focusing on 'problem' areas can lead to a shift in the dog's attitude (and your own) as training becomes less enjoyable. This may lead to a build-up of anxiety and pressure. It's a pattern that is easy to get sucked into, because we want to try to improve on the things we perceive as bad or weak. With this in mind, make time also to include the 'fun' things or the aspects that the dog is good at, so that there is relief, and the dog is able to receive plenty of positive reinforcement and enjoyment during the session.

Establish and Maintain Standards

Dogs thrive on consistency and a framework of rules to help them make sense of what we

A focused 'stay'. Here, quality is far more important than quantity.

want. It is better to reduce the level of difficulty of the task that you are working on than to reduce the standard of what you require. For example, when working on 'stay', being able to step one pace away from your dog while it maintains its position and great eye contact is of more value than being able to walk twenty paces away but the dog is gazing around everywhere except in your direction, and then as you go back to the dog it gets up and comes towards you. Or in the case of heelwork with a young puppy, a couple of steps in the correct heel position is far more desirable than a walk up the road with the pup pulling ahead on the lead.

The same goes for advanced fieldwork. Shortening the distance to get a great line to a retrieve, rather than accepting a poor line and then handling on regardless, will preserve what you are trying to achieve (a direct straight line). There are some exceptions to this case, but generally if it's a straightforward choice, always go for quality rather than quantity.

Enjoy the Art

Gundog training is very much an art as well as a science, and what science there is, is not exact. There are no equations or formulas that will help you produce the perfect working animal. Behavioural science can certainly help you with a methodology to train your dog (using the principles of positive reinforcement), but the art is in being able to read your dog, and quickly and accurately respond to what you see. And not only is there an art to reading your own dog but also to reading and responding to the current environmental conditions such as wind direction (and strength), terrain and barriers as they unfold.

5 STEADINESS AND NOISE ISSUES

Obedience is what you get from a dog that hasn't been tempted; steadiness is what you get from a dog that has overcome temptation.

JANET MENZIES (2010)

Much of the life of a working gundog is spent doing 'nothing', whether that is a retriever waiting patiently on the peg whilst his owner shoots, a spaniel dropping to flush and honouring a rabbit being shot on a walked-up day, a pointer going on point on the moor and maintaining that position while his handler and gun move into place, or a mixed team of dogs waiting well behind the gun lines ready to pick runners and sweep the woods after each drive. Patience is definitely a virtue when it comes to the life of a gundog – but equally we want them to switch on, with drive and commitment, when needed.

Young working-bred dogs in early training will likely be exuberant and full of energy, and you want to harness that passion, not extinguish it. Mental maturity will improve the dog's ability to act in a calmer way and manage its impulses, but you can't just expect that a dog's attitude and behaviour will improve with age. If a problem occurs in training, it is better to address it or backtrack what you are doing with the dog, and not just hope that he will 'grow out of it': they rarely do!

You will need to help your dog to learn how to control his own behaviour. This is more effective than trying to control the dog yourself, and can be done through established routines from an early age.

Make sure that you pick up some dummies so that your dog knows he will not have every retrieve.

Morse showed a lot of confidence as soon as Sara got him home, and he was not daunted by his two male house companions, an old Golden Retriever, Monty, and a black Labrador, Drummer. He was bold from the outset, and neither of the older dogs was disposed to disciplining him. It quickly became apparent that intervention from Sara would be needed to establish some boundaries in order to develop the best possible partnership with him.

Sara started by crate training Morse. Not only did this teach him to be content in his own company, but it also gave his house mates some much needed respite. He enjoyed his safe place, because it was a rewarding place to be, where he could enjoy a chew or a sleep. The crate in the car then became an extension to this, and Sara was able to train him to wait before getting out, both on his own, and in the company of the other two dogs. She also taught him to wait before being called to her for his dinner.

Sara gradually added distance and duration to some of Morse's sits, and also practised breaking up her heelwork and retrieves with periods of sitting quietly at heel 'doing nothing'. These were all opportunities for Morse to learn self-control and frustration tolerance, and that life wasn't all taking place in the fast lane. Sara then taught Morse to 'settle' in various locations, starting with lying on his own bed. This had the advantage of helping him to learn to switch off.

Sara kept her training and home life with Morse within a structured pattern, and made sure that she rewarded all good and calm behaviour. Importantly, she also ensured that he received no reward for being pushy, particularly around her other dogs. Gradually this helped him to develop his patience.

By learning to control his own impulses, Morse became much more reliable in the field when he was working. He had learnt that calm behaviour led to reward, and was able to manage any frustration he felt. Sara was very careful to understand her own dog's threshold, and to pick up on any displacement signs (such as yawning or scratching) if they happened, as this signified that Morse was becoming over-faced. She quickly distracted him from that behaviour, and rather than trying to complete the exercise that had built up to this, she broke away from the task and decided to revisit it later in the day or start afresh the next day.

Sara's ability to read Morse's behaviour was critical in understanding what he was feeling and how she should relate to this. She worked hard to establish a strong relationship whereby there was mutual trust, before trying to progress too far with his work in the field.

STEADINESS AND RUNNING IN

If you are training alone, several days a week, and teaching a young dog new concepts such as handling and lining, as well as marking, it is likely that you are necessarily giving that dog a lot of retrieves. Many drills will often involve repeating exercises, and before you know it, even in a short fifteen-minute session, the dog will have picked up several dummies, far more than he would do in an all-day group training session or competition. If you take the dog out on his own, it may not be long before that dog starts to think that every retrieve that is thrown or placed is for himself.

This is something to be aware of, and there are some strategies that you can employ to counteract that 'all mine' mentality. Occasionally you can go out and pick up a dummy yourself. This will give your dog a valuable break in proceedings, helping him to understand that it is not always his turn, and it will also ensure that you remain alert and mark things properly, which is a vital skill for any trainer. Alternatively, remember you don't have to pick every dummy that is thrown or placed. You can either leave it there to return to as a delayed retrieve, or collect it yourself at the end of the session.

If you have a dog that repeatedly runs in, the most important thing to ensure is that this behaviour does not keep getting rewarded. You will need to enlist some help to pick up the dummy quickly before the dog can get there. If you are training alone, then you are best advised either to put on a handling collar so that you can loosely hold the dog at heel, or let the dog trail a long line from a soft collar so that if it runs in, you can stand on the end of the line so the dog can only get so far before the line stops it.

'PUSH BEHAVIOUR' AT HEEL

Dogs that repeatedly run in before they are sent for a retrieve often show several signs of being unsteady and over-aroused before they actually leave the handler's side. This behaviour is usually built up over an extended time, and the early warning signs are either not noticed or they are ignored by the trainer. For example, some dogs may paddle their feet in anticipation of being sent for a retrieve, which is usually noticed once it gets pronounced – but often the precursor to this behaviour is taking just a single step forwards when the mark goes out. This small step is often not seen by the handler, or they think it is not worth paying attention to, and so the first cracks start to appear.

In fact the dog is exhibiting what can be termed as 'push behaviour', whereby it is 'pushing' its handler to be sent. In other instances, dogs rise up from a sit, not quite into a stand, so they appear to hover, suspended in a taut state. Again, the handler may ignore this or not be concerned about it as the dog hasn't actually run in, and looks as if it is remaining steady. In fact some handlers praise their dog for not running in and then allow them to retrieve as

Pay attention to pushy behaviour at heel, and don't reward it.

well, thus doubly rewarding the dog for its pushy behaviour.

Before a dog is sent for a retrieve it actually receives a whole chain of cues. For example, when you are going to send the dog for a blind retrieve you may step forwards and get it into a standing position. Next, you might look out to the point on the horizon where you want to send it, and check that its body is facing this direction in alignment, and that its head, and most importantly its eyes, are looking this way too. Then you might bring your hand down to point to the place you have picked out, checking again that the dog is now looking down through your hand towards the correct location – and then you will give a verbal cue to the dog to send it.

On a marked retrieve, there may be some additional and very different cues involved for the dog. In a group setting, the dog will have noticed the presence of a dummy thrower. He will see them fire a shot, which will draw his gaze, and then he will see the dummy being thrown and will see it land. The next cue they might expect is for you to send him on a vocal command. However, in a group training situation, the next cue that is likely to happen is the trainer saying your name, and so this becomes another cue to the dog. Likewise, in a working test the judge will tell you to send your dog, and again, this will form an additional layer to the hierarchy of cues. Alternatively, another shot may be fired and another dummy thrown, and the sequence will start again.

Training alone you have control over these cues and can isolate them so that the dog is responding as you want for success. That is, if you throw the dummy yourself, you will watch the dog to ensure that it maintains a still and steady position. If it does not, then you can deny the retrieve.

With a dog that is exhibiting any form of push behaviour, it is important that you understand all the cues that might be triggers for your dog's behaviour, and notice how your dog is responding to each of them. One client thought that it was the shot being fired that made the dog over-excited prior to the retrieve, but when we analysed the situation carefully it actually turned out to be the dummy thrower raising their arm prior to firing the shot and throwing the dummy that was triggering the dog and promoting it to start its push behaviour. This was something that the client was able to isolate easily, and with the help of a patient friend, could desensitise the dog before progressing with its training.

When you line up a dog to send it on a blind retrieve, if you see any form of over-arousal or over-investment in the retrieve prior to sending, then you can merely stand up again without sending the dog. If you repeat this pattern, the dog will learn what it has to do in order to earn the retrieve. If you see any form of undesired behaviour at the first cue then it is important not to allow the dog to proceed. Remember, there is no rush to send a dog to pick a canvas dummy: it can remain there until you get

the behaviours that you require. It is important that you don't just allow a pushy dog to rush you into sending it.

If you are also able to condition your dog to hear praise during the duration of his behaviour prior to retrieving, then he will understand that what he is doing is right, even if he is not being instantly rewarded with a retrieve. This will become important during group work, where not every retrieve will be offered to your own dog, despite him behaving appropriately. You can work up to the stage of the dog being able to hear your voice and praise, but not running in to fetch the retrieve, by firstly doing this with the dog in a 'stay' exercise or at heel without any retrieves.

MOVING ON FLUSH OR SHOT

A spaniel is required to drop to flush and shot when it locates a bird or rabbit. Taking a few steps or moving after the quarry comes under the same principle as above: the dog is exhibiting a push behaviour and is unsteady, but from a remote position, rather than be-

The spaniel must remain steady after flushing a bird.

This exercise is a simulation of something that might happen in a spaniel field trial. The handler at H1 has their spaniel out remotely from them, on the drop, because a bird has been shot behind their dog, which was flushed by the spaniel at the other end of the line, and shot for them. The dog must, therefore, sit steady in its remote position while the other dog is working to locate this bird. After a while the judge asks the handler (H1) to call their dog in to them, without using a whistle as this will interfere with the working of the other dog.

It then becomes clear that the other dog is not succeeding with the retrieve and it is called up, whereby the handler (H1) is asked to walk down to the other end of the line, with their dog, and will then be asked to make the retrieve from H2, which is where the other handler was working from.

This is a useful exercise to replicate as it will highlight various training elements, namely:

- Waiting quietly on the drop.
- Recalling (without whistle) to the handler with the distraction of a 'bird' behind.
- Walking away at heel to H2.
- Sending on an angle to an area where the dog may or may not have marked the bird.

To simulate this scenario on your own, you can leave your dog out remotely and throw your dummy over their head (as shown on the diagram). Then wait for one minute, ob-

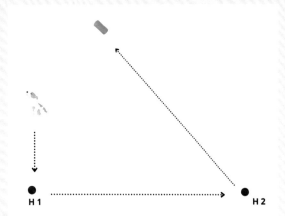

Diagram: simulated flush and retrieve exercise for a spaniel.

serving your dog's reactions. He may remain locked on to the dummy if he has watched you throw it. This is fine, but watch his body language: is he over-excited or pushy in his behaviour, or calm and still?

When you call the dog in, does he come immediately, or does he hesitate? Does he break for the retrieve? Or does he make a noise? When the dog has returned to you, will he walk calmly to heel up to the new sending position (H2)?

Next, line up the dog for the retrieve. Does he take the line as an angle to the retrieve, or does he pull to run back along the line he has just walked, and go to the mark from there? From this simple exercise, you should be able to unpick a few areas that need more work.

ing at the handler's side. The same procedure should be applied in that the dog should not be rewarded by being allowed to retrieve. Go out to the dog and reset it to the position it moved from. Return to your original place and then praise the dog for now being in the desired place. Offer the retrieve to somebody else if possible, and then either recall the dog to you or ask it to hunt on. When the dog does offer the desired behaviour of stopping to flush, ensure that you mark and reward this; you can also occasionally give the dog the retrieve as a reward but not always, so that it doesn't start to predict a pattern again.

NOISE ISSUES

The precursor to noise from the dog, as with steadiness issues, is usually the inability to deal with frustration. The dog vocalises its frustration at not being able to gain an instant reward or gratification, such as a retrieve. Usually this is because it does not understand the feeling of frustration, as it has not been educated to deal with it. It is very important that frustration tolerance is built into your early routines with a young dog. If you invest time in teaching your dog how to deal with small amounts of frustration, then this will also help to teach it to be more patient and to think before it reacts.

You will need to help your dog to learn to manage its behaviour in the face of increasing arousal and distraction. This is something that must be built carefully and considerately over time, first by working on self-management at home and alone, and then by introducing other dogs into the equation – but in so

Waiting patiently to be called out of the kennel.

doing reducing the stimulation. For example, your dog may sit steadily while you throw a mark at home, not run in, and not make any noise on the outrun when sent – but when you replicate this in company with additional dogs it becomes noisy. Therefore, in the first group outings, rather than putting your dog in this situation and expecting it to be quiet while other dogs retrieve, try to do some group obedience work instead. This will give your dog exposure to a group of other dogs but doing less exciting work. Only when your dog is able to work calmly in the company of other dogs in this manner can you then think about introducing retrieve work in a group setting.

Noise issues are often exacerbated when the dog is working in company and expected to watch other dogs working, whilst remaining calm and steady itself. Heightened arousal or excitement is not an uncommon issue when you make the leap from training alone to expecting your dog to work in the company of other dogs (and handlers). And it can be extremely frustrating when you feel that you have done all the garden heelwork exercises, solo retrieve work and drill sessions, and the dog appears to be managing itself appropriately, only to find that it 'boils over' in company. But the move into a group situation, with the competition of other dogs, and the stimulation of fresh new ground and retrieving opportunities, means that excitement levels are increased considerably. So how can you tackle this? To be completely successful, you will need to apply a two-pronged attack process, combining continued quality work alone, with repeated group outings to put the dog back into the situation.

At Home

The mainstay of your conditioning and maintenance work on frustration tolerance can be done at home, where you can set up exercises that help your dog manage its impulses and maintain its self-control. Ensure that you notice relaxed behaviour in the face of distractions, not just the dog maintaining a position. There is a very important, but subtle, difference. For example, be careful not to praise a sit where ac-

The competition of other dogs in group work can exacerbate arousal levels in some dogs.

tually the dog is over-aroused and poised for action, panting or hovering. You may inadvertently be reinforcing a behaviour that you don't want or which is undesirable.

If you have other dogs in your household, you can set up exercises that require waiting and patience, before the dog is called to you, or before an activity, but also maintaining a calm demeanour or position. For example, I have got a young pup now (coming up to eight months old) that is very 'full on'. I have just started taking her out on a morning walk with the big dogs, and require her to walk calmly at heel with me, on the lead, while the older dogs run free. She has found this challenging so far. When she first comes out of the kennel she is understandably excited, as are the older dogs. But she then settles into a more relaxed walk, holding a heel position, and I maintain this with praise and reward. And I will let her go off to play or sniff when I feel she is most relaxed or disengaged from the actions of the other dogs.

Another useful home technique is to video yourself frequently to watch for any tell-tale signs of push

behaviour from your dog whilst you are training. This can be as subtle as just the movement of the back feet when lining up the dog to send it, and you may not notice this at all when working alone. If you don't have access to video recording, then ask a friend or partner to watch you and your dog critically as you take a few retrieves; get them to note exactly how the

Using video to record and rewatch behaviours is useful to improve your understanding.

dog is relating to each exercise – its body position, actions, even its mouth, ear and tail positions. Their objective observations may well be enlightening, and you can then use this information to work on areas that need improvement.

In the Group

It is important to understand the type of noise a dog is making, or rather, why it is making noise, in a group scenario. Over-arousal or over-investment in the re-trieves that are happening leading to vocalisation is very different to 'puppy boredom' whines or yawns – almost the opposite in fact. I am far less concerned about a young pup that makes a little boredom noise after it has been sitting around for a long time in a group lesson, than I am about the dog that is vocalis-ing because it can't contain its excitement.

The beginning of any group situation is often the time when arousal and excitement is at its height, as the dog is often literally 'fresh out of the box'. Watch for signs of over-investment in the action, or a dog that is obsessing at the dummy thrower at the cost of being able to do anything else (such as turn away towards a blind). This may mean that you do nothing else other than observe, monitor and give feedback to your dog in the first twenty minutes of the lesson – but this is time very well spent.

Group sessions for puppies need careful management to ensure young dogs benefit from them.

Identify the Triggers

Work out what specifically winds up your dog. Is it the dummy being thrown? A shot being fired? Or an-other dog being sent? It may be all three! But I have seen students that think it is one thing, when it is ac-tually quite another. Knowing the triggers will help. For example, for a recent client I quickly realised that for her dog it was the shot being fired that triggered over-arousal and a response of jumping forwards from heel: every time a shot was fired the dog was linking this to the anticipation of a retrieve and was therefore 'pushing' to get ready. The shot was the first trigger for the dog. This gave the client some-thing simple to work on in isolation at home: de-sensitisation to the shot. This handler was able to go home and practise walking up and just firing a shot and then walking on again. She repeated this activity multiple times before introducing anything else into the chain, so that after a lot of work, the shot was no longer a cue to leap forwards.

For many dogs it is the sight of multiple retrieves being thrown, and then the addition of other dogs being sent for them, that pushes them over the edge. This is especially true for dogs that are good markers and very driven to retrieve. Group work, for them, can be partic-ularly frustrating. Look at it from their point of view: if they have learnt the rules for being sent on a marked retrieve – when a mark is thrown out they remain quiet, still, focused, locked on – and have fulfilled them, then it is not surprising that they become agitated to find they are not being sent for the retrieves that they have marked, and worse still another dog is being sent for them instead! The dog will feel that it has met all the usual criteria to be sent for the retrieve, had it been at home with the handler alone. But in company, not every retrieve that it marks in this way will be given to it. This is likely to exacerbate frustration, which in turn may lead to vocalisation as a release.

With this in mind, it is very important to endorse a dog positively for marking when it is in a group, so that it understands that it is still doing the right thing, and is rewarded for it – albeit not with a retrieve in every instance now.

Using Distraction to Break a Habit

In a group situation you will need to monitor your dog and how it is relating to the marks that are being thrown. If you can quietly praise your dog for marking the retrieves, then this will let him know that he is being rewarded for this behaviour, even though he is not being sent for each retrieve. If you feel that your dog is getting obsessed with marking, then try to interrupt this behaviour – so you allow it to mark briefly, but then distract it to look at you, and reward it with food or a toy. You may end up temporarily losing your 'lock on' to marks, but it is more important to ensure the dog is able to manage its behaviour and not becoming obsessed with marking.

For a dog that has started to make noise in group training when another dog is sent, again praise the dog for marking/locking on, but then quickly interrupt its attention and distract it as the other dog is sent, so that it doesn't spend a lot of time getting engrossed in the action. A pocketful of really tasty treats is useful here. The sequence is this: the dummy is thrown out; let the dog mark it; praise it; and then as another dog is sent, distract its head away with a piece of sausage (or whatever).

Start doing this for absolutely every retrieve in the group before the dog has a chance to vocalise. Your aim is to break its habit of getting over-invested and whining. This can eventually have the undesired outcome of the dog looking to you for reinforcement each time a marked retrieve goes out – but this is a temporary shift, and is far better than the dog seeing a mark and another dog going out and then squeaking. You will have broken the noise-cycle habit, but will have created a new habit of looking away or losing focus on the mark. However, you can gradually build back the marking and the 'lock on' as the dog learns to manage its impulses and to tolerate the routines of group training better. In Chapter 8 we revisit marking issues.

Maintain Consistency

Maintaining consistency is crucial. In group training there is often a tendency to rush. You may feel as if you are holding up other people, or you feel obliged

The handler rewards the dog for looking away while another dog retrieves.

to pick all the retrieves you are offered. However, try not to slip into this habit. Be consistent in what you require from your dog and what you are trying to achieve. Don't let things slide, otherwise you will end up reinforcing the dog for the very thing you didn't want it to do. That's not training – or rather, it is, but not the sort you want.

Look on your limited group sessions as a really valuable opportunity to be able to set up the dog and rehearse the things that you can't do alone, at home.

Don't Overdo Group Outings

Group training is fun – particularly for humans! You do need to do it, as we all need our dogs to operate in company, whether that is ultimately in the shooting field or in competition in a test or trial. And it is often a very pleasant social occasion. But the majority of your training should be done outside the group, to condition foundation behaviours until they are solid enough to withstand group outings.

If you are attending a lot of group sessions, but aren't prepared to focus fully on your own dog and any issues it is having with over-arousal, then you

Group training is usually a social and fun activity.

will quickly find that these sessions are becoming counterproductive, and all you are doing is encouraging a fully fledged noise or an over-aroused habit.

Vocalising on the Outrun: Marked Retrieves

It is important to look at, and understand, what causes a dog to make noise when it is sent for a marked retrieve, so that you can deal with it and eventually decrease or remove the unwanted behaviour.

It is likely that this is a keen dog and that it has become over-invested in the retrieve without the handler realising. As part of your training on marked retrieves, you will have made the effort to teach your dog to 'lock on' to marks when they are thrown. You want the dog to stay staring at the dummy, and if they do so (and fulfil other criteria) then they will be sent for the retrieve. This builds a staring habit, which gets rewarded. However, it is important to ensure that this staring habit doesn't become obsessive.

In your training at home by all means practise 'locking on' to marks, but also practise 'locking off', in that when you turn away from the mark and walk away the dog is prepared to come straightaway with you at heel. You can then delay gratification by sending the dog back for the memory blind if it has locked off and maintained good heelwork. We will discuss this in more detail in Chapter 8.

When you send your dog for a mark and you think there is a danger that it may vocalise on the way out, the most important thing is that the dog doesn't get the reward of the retrieve if it does make a noise. Therefore you need to enlist the help of somebody to pick up the dummy when this happens, or be able to vocally stop your dog from continuing. If your dog makes a noise on the outrun, this is one of the few occasions when I would recommend immediately vocally 'correcting' the dog with 'No!'. What this does is clearly mark the behaviour immediately as inappropriate and wrong, at the precise moment. This should help the dog to build the correlation that what it did at that moment is not going to lead to a reward, and the reason for there being no subsequent retrieve.

Equally importantly, if you are working on this issue, then you need to quietly praise the dog on its outrun as it leaves your side without making any noise, to endorse the behaviour as desirable. This lets the dog know that this is what you want, and in turn, it will get the reward of the retrieve as well.

If you are absolutely consistent with this approach – denying retrieves when there is noise; praising when the dog is running quietly; using techniques of distraction where necessary in a group; and improving self-management when alone – you will be able to overcome this issue.

Water work can often increase arousal levels.

Andrew had been careful to take things very cautiously with his young flatcoat bitch, Sadie, as she initially made a noise on marked retrieves. He kept the excitement levels down by just giving her memory marks when she was quiet, and at the end of the training session she was then able to have a direct mark without making a noise. But all of this was done alone, and once she went into company the noise started once more. Again, he made slow and careful progress by going right back to basics and getting her to do just obedience behaviours around another dog, then gradually reintroduced the retrieve into the equation. With patience, after several months of work, she was able to stay quiet and calm to any thrown mark and whilst honouring other dogs working.

However, when Andrew tried to introduce water retrieves, noise began to start again and this pushed Sadie into an even deeper state of excitement. He worked on this issue by desensitising her to the splash of a dummy in a paddling pool. Then he moved to larger stretches of water, where he used a dummy thrown in on a string, which could be brought back to shore without her retrieving. He combined this approach with the use of a clicker and reward for quiet, calm behaviour around the water.

To build a successful quiet habit around water, we next removed the retrieving element and worked instead on recalls over water towards Andrew, ensuring that Sadie had a good response to returning to him directly over water, and rewarding her when she returned quickly and quietly. Next we were able to introduce the dummy into this pattern by putting it on the edge of the water near Andrew, so again Sadie was recalled across the water and on to the dummy before returning to him. By not throwing the dummy and not sending Sadie on an outrun, we had eliminated the most exciting elements of the retrieve. Gradually we put the dummy further into the pond, still recalling Sadie on to it.

When we had built up a pattern of quiet retrieves towards us in this way, we then reintroduced the outrun. We placed the dummy into the edge of the water, with Sadie at heel, and then walked away from the bank to use the dummy as a memory blind retrieve. With the retrieve being delayed, and only a small element of water involved, this was a much less exciting set-up for Sadie than a marked retrieve. We were careful to ensure that Andrew and Sadie were a good distance away from the water before sending Sadie back for the retrieve, so that if she did vocalise on the outrun she could be stopped before she got to the bank, or we could remove the dummy from the water before she reached it. This way, there was no reward for any over-aroused behaviour.

Next we placed a memory mark retrieve over the water. Sadie watched with interest as the dummy was placed on the far bank, and then Andrew heeled her away as before and she was able to complete the retrieve over water when she was quiet. With this systematic approach, Andrew and Sadie were eventually able to build towards marked retrieves both over and on water. It took a lot of time and patience, but because the work had been methodical, it helped Sadie to understand how she would be rewarded with the retrieve, and she was able to manage her own arousal level.

Heeling away will help to ensure your dog does not become over-invested in marked retrieves.

Vocalising on the Outrun: Blind Retrieves

Noise made on blind retrieves is a slightly less common issue, and one that happens for an entirely different reason to noise made on marked retrieves. Usually it has nothing to do with over-excitement, over-arousal or over-investment in the retrieve, and is primarily down to a degree of anxiety, confusion or pressure being felt by the dog, when you enter into your set-up for a blind retrieve.

The dog is not confident or clear about what it is being asked to do. Sometimes the dog will 'no go' or curl into the handler's side to avoid being sent in these circumstances. When the dog does go out, it can end up vocalising through uncertainty. This is often more prevalent when a marked diversion is put into the mix. For example, on a straightforward blind the dog may not make a noise, but go out with reduced power (again demonstrating its lack of confidence), whereas when a marked retrieve is added into the scenario, the dog will go for the blind but vocalise as a way of expressing its anxiety or uncertainty. In this respect, the dog understands that it shouldn't be going for the mark (as it recognises the cues to an extent), but it is not completely confident of what it should be doing instead.

If this has crept into your dog's work, it is important to acknowledge it, and to deal with it in a timely fashion so that it does not become an ingrained habit.

As with any vocalisation on the outrun, do not let the dog proceed, mark the behaviour as inappropriate, deny the retrieve, and bring the dog back in straightaway. You don't want to inadvertently reward the dog for making noise, although you may be happy that it has taken your line to pick the blind.

Rather than resetting the whole exercise, which is beyond the dog's remit at this stage, you should backtrack and do some work on improving confidence in blinds instead. You need to re-cement the association between your set-up for a blind, and the dog going in that direction and being successful. This may mean a period of working on trailing memory blinds, sight blinds or comfort area blinds, before proceeding again to more complex set-ups. In Chapter 7 we will look in more detail at some of the issues that can occur when lining for blind retrieves, and how more confident outruns can be established.

When you are ready to go back to putting the diversion mark back into the set-up, you should go through a period of picking this first, before the blind, so that this is removed from the equation. Once the dog is doing this successfully, then you can revert to picking a blind first before the distraction mark, but ensure that you make the angle and distance between the two significant, so that no doubt about your requirements will seep into the dog's mind.

PULLING FORWARDS AT HEEL

Dogs that take part in walked-up shooting or dummy training soon start to learn the routine, and understand that all the exciting action is usually taking place 'out front'. This can lead to them pulling forwards at heel, to get a better mark or in anticipation of being sent for a retrieve. As with the previously described push behaviour at heel, it is important that this pulling ahead is not rewarded.

Use two approaches to improve your heelwork. First, revert to practising heelwork in a less stimulating environment so that you can rehearse good behaviour and ensure that this is rewarded. This may mean going right back to working on heel position indoors, before taking it back outside again. Ensure that the dog is aware of where the desired position is in relation to your left leg, and reward him for trying to stay in contact with that leg. In this respect you are developing his 'left leg awareness' so that he is actively tracking where that leg is going and following it. You can develop this by doing some turns at heel and changes of pace, and even trying to do a mini-'dressage' type course on your lawn or piece of bare ground.

Don't rush through this work. You are trying to re-ingrain a good heelwork habit. Be super critical. If you don't have perfect heelwork at home, under minimal distraction, then you will have little chance of having acceptable heelwork once the environment becomes much more rewarding.

Next, when you revisit walked-up group work, monitor your dog and how it is relating. If it is a training session, ask to not have any retrieves for the first half-hour (or however long you need) so that you don't have to worry about marking anything, and can concentrate fully on your dog and how he is now behaving in this situation. If the dog is pulling forwards you will not be letting it have any retrieves at all. This behaviour will receive no reward. Keep monitoring the dog until it starts to settle. This may take some time, but it is important that the dog does not get sent for any retrieves until it is in the desired heel position. You can also use a handling collar or

Poor heelwork can soon become ingrained if it is ignored.

lead to maintain the dog in the correct position while he relearns the new behaviour.

When your dog is in the correct position, ensure that you mark this and reward him. If you are happy that this behaviour is consistent, then let him have a retrieve. This work will require patience and consistency from you, so that you help the dog to understand the pattern of what leads to reward.

Reward good heelwork in low distraction environments to reset a good habit.

6 RECALL AND DELIVERY ISSUES

Return and delivery are where the majority of issues are seen with retrieve training. Most well-bred gundogs will be happy to run out to a thrown dummy that they have seen. They enjoy the chase part of the retrieve as this links to a natural ability and their prey drive. However, returning and handing over their quarry can often be a weakness. If you relate this to a wild instinct behaviour then the retrieve has evolved from a chase-catch-kill-eat pattern to a chase-catch-bring it back-give it up pattern. The latter parts of this chain do not really offer the dog much reward, whereas the early parts are still very exciting and rewarding. Unfortunately, without a return and delivery you don't have a retrieve.

For the dog to want to bring you the retrieve item, you will need to have established a good relationship and bond first, and a strong recall response. If your standalone recall is not strong, then you don't stand much chance of your recall being solid once a retrieve is introduced into the equation. Practise a strong recall in multiple locations with a worthwhile reward (for the dog) before reintroducing the retrieve.

Use the reward that your dog enjoys most to speed up recalls.

SLOW RETURNS

Hunting for, and locating, the retrieve is very rewarding for most gundogs, but for some, that is where the enjoyment ends. Bringing the retrieve back to their handler doesn't offer them anything extra. In these cases, you will sometimes see dogs returning slowly with no real purpose or sense of urgency. To combat this, it is necessary to think of making the delivery much more rewarding for the dog. What does your dog enjoy most? Is there a tasty food treat that would motivate him, or would the chance to play with a reward ball or toy do the trick? Or, you can give the dog the opportunity to chase you. This will help to reset a new pattern, where coming back to you is as much fun as leaving.

SWAPPING RETRIEVES AND 'HUNTING ON'

The behaviour that you want when your dog finds a retrieve is for him to bring it straight back to you. But if you are practising drill retrieves where you have placed more than one dummy out in an area, or you are in a group situation where the trainer has put several retrieves out, then you may find that your dog is faced with temptation, and instead of returning quickly to you decides to 'shop around' the pile of dummies, or swap the one it has picked for another that it unexpectedly comes across. Also, some dogs that are unchecked, will pick the retrieve and continue to engage in the hunting behaviour ('hunting on'),

MAKING RETURNS MORE FUN

Sam was an adolescent Golden Retriever, who was keen to retrieve but lost focus and interest once he had located the dummy. He would usually pick it up, but would then meander back to his owner with no drive or consistency, sometimes even stopping to cock his leg on the return, too. The situation appeared to be worse when his handler was in a group.

Working with his owner, Lynn, we used two strategies to ensure that returning was extremely rewarding. First, we started taking Sam's food bowl out into the field with him, and putting a small portion of his dinner in it prior to each of his retrieves. Lynn then cast him off for the retrieve, and once he had picked up, she placed the food bowl on the ground in front of her. Sam saw this and sped towards her to get his dinner. Obviously this meant spitting the dummy out to eat, but because we were working on returns we weren't worried about this. His delivery had not been a point of concern before, and we knew we could make this good again in due course, if necessary, once we had improved the returns. The important thing was that he was reward-ed for fast returns. If there were any returns that were not quick, then Lynn could simply pick the bowl up again before he reached it, and so he was not rewarded. This was very effective, and gradually we were able to move the food bowl to behind her, and then eventually fade it out completely and swap it for a hand-fed reward after delivery.

The other thing that we worked on was Lynn's presence in group situations. Being a novice handler, she didn't feel confident enough to make herself more exciting and interesting to come back to. The young dog was dealing with the pressure of returning to a big group, and was rightly feeling a measure of trepidation, which could have been eased by Lynn coming out of the line of other handlers and by introducing some fun and excitement. A few 'whoop, whoop' calls, and getting the dog to chase her as she ran away, soon turned the second part of the retrieve into an even bigger game for both of them. Sam forgot his anxiety about the other handlers and dogs as he focused on catching up with Lynn.

Several dummies in one location may provide too much temptation to swap for some dogs.

sometimes moving further away from their handlers, as this is a rewarding activity for the dog. In both cases, the dog is thinking more of its own self-gratification and less of returning quickly to its handler.

Early on in the young dog's schooling, you may decide to ignore any swapping behaviour you witness as you don't want to dampen the dog's enthusiasm for retrieving, but at some point you will need to address it before it becomes an ingrained habit. However, this should be done with caution. Sending the dog out to a nearby pile of dummies and then telling it off as it goes to swap may mean that the dog is reluctant to go back to that area again at all, or it may return there and pick nothing, standing staring at you, as it thinks it has been told off for picking something up.

When you decide to address the swapping problem, it needs to be done with some thought as to the stimuli that the dog is receiving to retrieve (both visual and scent) and with great care in your timing of any praise or correction. Before you attempt this exercise, ensure that your dog is comfortable with hearing verbal praise while it is working – 'good lad' or 'good girl' – and also understands a vocal correction such as 'ah, ah' or 'no', which predicts non-reward for undesirable behaviour. Check that these both work and that you can switch between them comfortably, using a distinct change to the tone of your voice in each case. There is no need to shout, just alter your tone. Being able to time your praise and vocal correction perfectly is also very important. Alternatively, if you don't want to use any vocal correction for this exercise, and your dog has been conditioned, you can give a positive vocal interrupter, such as 'pup, pup', 'enough' or 'with me' – something that will get your dog's focus back on yourself.

With an ingrained swapping habit, don't aim to 'fix' it all in one day, but rather break down this training into separate sessions over the course of some weeks. For the first exercise, you will need two visual dummies (preferably with white on them) that the dog can clearly see on some bare ground. Walking into the wind, take the dog with you and put out one

When working on swapping, ensure that the dummies are placed with adequate distance between them.

dummy at about 30 metres. If you can, stand it up on its end for maximum visibility. This will be the back dummy. Then return with your dog about twenty metres and position another white dummy similarly. Then return the remaining ten metres and turn to face the two in-line dummies.

Line up the dog and send him to pick the nearest dummy. He will be able to see both of these dummies, but there is a good distance between them. This is important. Because of the wind he will also be getting a scent stimulus from both. As your dog reaches the first dummy and puts his mouth around it, be ready to give him feedback on his next decision and actions. If he picks and returns straightaway, then praise him as soon as he has made that commitment: he has made a good decision.

However, if he picks the first dummy and then doesn't return with it immediately, you need to be ready to give him a vocal correction (or use your positive vocal interruptor) to mark his incorrect choice. This lets the dog know that he should be doing something else, and gets him to focus back on you. The behaviours your dog might choose are these: picking one dummy, then heading towards the other dummy to investigate (hunting on); picking one dummy and then going to swap it with the other one; or picking one dummy and then trying to get the other one in his mouth as well.

Having the second dummy a good distance away will give you time to watch the dog's behaviour and to mark it as either correct or incorrect accordingly. With a very vocally responsive dog, it is likely that you will be able to avert the swapping behaviour with your vocal sound before he gets to the other dummy. In which case you will then need to quickly switch back to praising him for returning to you as you initially wanted.

If your dog does succeed in swapping, ignoring your vocal correction and returning with the swapped dummy, do not correct him for bringing it back to you as this will only confuse the dog, and may

Once the dog has picked the first dummy, praise him for returning quickly, or interrupt him from continuing on to pick another dummy.

BURIED TREASURE

Geoff's Cocker Ginny had developed an interesting trait that is sometimes seen with Cockers: she was trying to bury the retrieve after she had found it! Whilst this was amusing to witness at first, it is obviously undesirable and needed to be rectified with care. First we made sure that Ginny didn't do any more retrieves where there would be an opportunity for her to repeat this behaviour. We wanted to break the habit.

Next we took her on to Geoff's driveway where there were few scent distractions and nowhere for her to think about hiding a retrieve. Here we just began by doing some simple recalls to Geoff, with no retrieve, and used food treats and praise to reward her for coming straight back. We kept the distances very short in the first instance, and encouraged good eye contact from Ginny once she returned to Geoff and sat in front of him.

Next we introduced a small dummy, using the same distraction-free environment. We only threw the dummy a short distance and Geoff crouched down as Ginny picked and turned towards him, to ensure he encouraged her to come all the way back in to him. He made a fuss of Ginny when she presented the retrieve and didn't rush to take it off her, but gave her plenty of praise for bringing it in.

Once this behaviour was reliable, Geoff was then able to take Ginny on to some short grass and go through the same steps, doing some straightforward recalls first for food rewards, and then moving on to short retrieves as before. He kept the distances short again to ensure ready success. Once this stage was consistent, Geoff was able to start increasing the distances for Ginny's retrieves and start working in more distracting environments.

Working at a short distance on bare ground to ensure success.

---

also result in later delivery issues. You will only use your vocal correction when he is attempting to swap. Just take the dummy from him and reset the exercise, but either ensure you send him from a closer distance, or ensure the back dummy is further away so that the next time you achieve success.

If you are uncomfortable with using a vocal correction or interruptor with your dog, then you can do this exercise using a helper positioned ready to pick up the back dummy if your dog decides to move towards it. This way the dog cannot self-reward for its action of hunting on. You will simply praise the dog if he picks the first dummy and commits to returning, and ignore him when he tries to swap, and reset the exercise.

Once your dog has successfully retrieved the front dummy, then send him back to pick the other one. This will aid his learning that he is not being denied the other retrieve, but that he has to pick one and return with it before he is able to pick the other one.

You may need to repeat this exercise a couple of times if your dog has attempted to swap so that you can emphasise the praise when he gets it right. Also, remember to praise the return on the second retrieve as well if you are happy with it. In addition, if you have had to repeat this exercise a few times due to errors, it is a good idea to revert to just sending out for a single dummy so that you can consolidate success. You also want to ensure that drive is maintained.

Building from this exercise, in later weeks, you can change the visual and scent stimulus combinations that the dog is getting, by using different coloured dummies and varying the wind direction. For example, use a white dummy for the front retrieve and a green or non-visual dummy for the back retrieve. This way the dog will pick the first dummy and have no visual pull for the second dummy, but he will receive a scent stimulus if he is working into the wind. This may provoke the dog to investigate just as much, and in some cases more, than a visual draw. Then try both dummies as non-visual to see how your dog responds, again into wind, before trying both dummies as white targets but working downwind.

You will learn a lot from watching how your dog responds in each of these situations. Ultimately you want the dog to pick just the first dummy that he finds and return directly to you.

As an advanced adaptation of this exercise, find a piece of ground with some cover, and pre-plant a blind in the cover. Your dog will not know about this retrieve. Then throw a short mark for your dog, so that when he picks this retrieve he will be in an area where he will wind the second retrieve but cannot see it. This may provoke the desire to hunt on for this other retrieve. Again, monitor the dog's behaviour and respond accordingly with vocal feedback in a timely manner.

Whilst it is important to address the issues of swapping and hunting on, particularly if you are going to compete in field trials, as it is an eliminating fault, you also need to be careful not to overdo these exercises as it could have an adverse effect on the dog's drive and confidence if you need to reset or vocally correct him.

Delivery with the head turning away, trying to retain the dummy, or jumping up are some of the undesirable forms of delivery.

A young dog will often pick up the dummy and carry it using the toggle or rope.

DELIVERY ISSUES

There seems to be a myriad of ways that delivery can disappoint! Ideally you want delivery of the retrieve with the dog's head up, to front, and presented tenderly to hand. The undesirable variations include fly-pasts, stay-aways and parading with the dummy, and then there are those that drop, those that hang on, those that fumble and those that seem to have difficulty carrying altogether. Others turn their head away, jump up, or insist on carrying the dummy by its end or by the toggle. Mouthing and messing with game complete the list of potential misdemeanours – and that's before you have added delivery from water into the mix.

Physical Difficulties

Some of the difficulties experienced by a dog in holding on to dummies or game can be as a result of its stature or strength. For example, a small working-bred Cocker with its tiny jaw will manage only a certain size of gape when it opens its mouth, and therefore isn't physically able to hold very large items

Carrying a large game bird or hare can provide a physical challenge to a small spaniel.

The large dummy gives the dog practice in widening its gape.

string, can be helped by giving it a larger sized but lightweight dummy. This will get it to open its mouth more, encouraging a better central hold.

By working on improving both gape and strength, you should be able to improve the consistency in your dog's hold and carriage.

Parading, Fly Pasts and Keep-Aways

Parading, fly pasts and keep-aways are behaviours that partly infuriate and partly amuse handlers. A dog goofing around with the dummy, staying away, doing a 'victory loop' or flinging it about looks as if it is having a great time. It probably is. This sort of game can be highly rewarding for the dog, as it explores the novelty of the retrieve article and plays its own game. Contrast this to just bringing the dummy back to hand over to its handler, who is now displeased, and you can see why this behaviour starts to self-perpetuate.

However, as well as being playful, some 'keep away' behaviour is fearful and can be caused by a handler who has told the dog off for some part of its return. It may be that the deliveries were not as desired and the handler has expressed displeasure at this, but the dog has interpreted the handler's reaction as being one of general displeasure when it comes back with

unless it develops a technique for doing so, such as carrying a heavy pheasant cock bird by the neck or wing. Also, tiredness often plays a role in the dog's ability to carry its retrieves correctly. If the dog has been given a lot of work on long retrieves, or a spaniel has had some lengthy hunts, then these are the times when you may see further deterioration in the dog's ability to hold on to and carry its retrieves.

Some difficulties with carrying larger items of game result from a lack of strength of the dog's jaw or neck muscles. This can be improved with some weight-lifting practice, with heavier weight dummies or by asking the dog to carry a small log. Another way of strengthening the dog's muscles in this respect is to give it a good-sized knuckle bone or natural root to chew periodically. This will work the jaw and neck muscles and help towards overall strength conditioning.

A dog that fumbles or is loose-mouthed with a smaller sized dummy, or that picks by the toggle or

A dog that won't deliver to hand, but flies past the handler instead, causes frustration.

the retrieve article. Therefore it is easy to see why the dog becomes reluctant to return. Many handlers resort to using a barrier method to prevent these fly-pasts, such as standing with their back to a fence or wall, or putting the dog on a long line. However, as soon as they are back out in the open again, the issue is still there, and the dog returns to 'showboating'. The problem with employing the 'barrier' methods described above is that they just prevent the dog doing the behaviour at the time, but they don't actually remove the desire to do the behaviour: they remove the dog's ability to do the physical action, but leave the mindset for the activity still firmly in place.

To deal with the issue successfully, it is important to understand why the dog is parading with the dummy or running around the handler. Understanding what lies behind the behaviour will help you to tackle it effectively. There may be a number of reasons, and the solutions in each case would be subtly, or sometimes significantly, different. Some things that might be considered are described below.

Over-Excitement, Over-Exuberance, Over-Stimulation

Sometimes the dog finds the retrieve highly exciting. It stimulates his chase and prey drive to such an extent that he can't manage and control his behaviour to offer the calm return and delivery that is required. In this case the dog is more likely to exhibit the behaviour on single marked retrieves, or at the beginning of the training session, when its adrenalin is high.

If this is the case, then first work on recalls without the dummy. Put the dog remotely in the field and recall him to you. Then you will need to restart training the recall with the dummy. You can do this by sitting the dog out remotely and placing the dummy right near your feet. Recall the dog and praise him for coming back quickly. Let him pick the dummy up as he gets to you. Praise him and then take the dummy immediately whilst praising him for delivering it. This sequence will give him every opportunity to get the return and delivery as you want it. Gradually work the dummy back, further away from you, once the delivery is reliable.

Place the dummy very close to you, so that the dog picks and delivers almost at once.

Don't be tempted to put the dummy halfway between your dog and yourself until you have achieved several repetitions of the sequence above. Just move the dummy gradually away from you on subsequent repetitions. You want to practise and repeat success so that the dog is recalling strongly towards you, picking up the dummy and placing it in your hand. The less time the dog spends with the dummy initially the better, as there will be less time for things to go wrong. All the time the dog is doing what you want (not playing with the dummy or running around with it) you should praise him. If you do push ahead too quickly and the dog starts to revert to the undesired behaviour, then you need to backtrack and practise several more repetitions of him getting it right. This will help to cement the pattern in the dog's mind.

When working in a group training situation, ask not to have a marked retrieve as your first retrieve, but rather have a very delayed memory or a blind retrieve. Or take your dog out, leave him statically and cast him left or right on to the retrieve, so that you are putting in some control first and the dog is working with you, and you have removed the exciting 'chase' element of the retrieve.

In dealing with this sort of over-aroused return behaviour, quietly praise your dog for the good return, but as soon as he goes to deviate from delivering to you or he starts to move off elsewhere you need to quickly mark this behaviour with a vocal interruptor, which should get his attention back on you again. Then praise again if his focus comes back to you, so he can understand the difference, and what you require. If his attention doesn't come back to you, then it would be best to go and collect the dog, and then reset the return behaviour, without the dummy, rewarding him for a good return to the delivery position.

Working in Company

Often it is the distraction or competition of other dogs that will affect the dog's retrieve. A dog that is not used to other dogs, and is not well socialised (or

A dog may feel 'line pressure' running towards a group of handlers and other dogs.

is over social), will find working in the company of other dogs challenging. Sometimes handlers are in a rush to get their dogs out in company, but it can be too much, too soon. If working with other dogs is too distracting or exciting, then again, lower the criteria so that you expect less from your dog in company. Go back to just doing some strong recalls towards you and the other dogs, for high-value food rewards, so that the dog is reinforced for coming back quickly, strongly and directly. Monitor how your dog is relating to the situation and try to capture any calm and steady behaviour and reward it.

It may also help to join a different dog activity group (such as obedience or rally obedience) where you can get used to working your dog around other dogs, so that this becomes less of a novelty or distraction.

Line Pressure (Handler-Induced Pressure)

Standing off from you, playing keep-away, or parading at a distance can also be the dog's response to feeling 'line pressure': that is, he feels pressurised either by his own handler (because you have had delivery problems in the past), or by the presence of other people and dogs in the group or line. Dogs that feel line pressure may start to exhibit slow returns as they get nearer to you. They may stop, reposition the dummy, or start to mouth or bite down on the dummy.

For this sort of issue you need to make the retrieve less formal, and not pressure the dog into giving you a delivery. If you can praise the dog when it is coming back fast, that will help, so it understands what is desired. Also, try not to eyeball the dog. A number of people (and dogs) staring at a returning dog can be very off-putting. Once the dog has picked, you could try turning and moving away from your dog, so it has to follow you. You can also let it come into heel instead of to your front, which will relieve eye-to-eye

ASHLEY AND INDIA: DELIVERY CHALLENGES

Ashley describes her Labrador India as fizzy, high drive, intelligent and prone to over-arousal. She is Ashley's first gundog and by her own admission she has made lots of mistakes along the way, which have mostly been remedied over time. In the past she used to bark at shot, and ran in repeatedly on marked retrieves.

In high stress or new or exciting situations, such as walked-up scenarios with unfamiliar dogs or with water, she will not give up the dummy at the end of the retrieve. She will also shake it, or hold it tight and parade around with it. It doesn't happen every time, and if there are multiple dummies involved in the retrieve scenario then she delivers well, and if the exercise is made harder then she is also much better.

Ashley was frustrated and was feeling rather desperate about the situation, but I reminded her just how much progress and success she had enjoyed so far with India. Sometimes it is easy to lose sight of this. She had overcome some significant issues, so I was confident that with consistency she would be able to face up to this challenge also.

There were some key points to be noted:
- India did this behaviour under high arousal.
- She didn't do it if there was more of a challenge in the retrieve or if there were multiple retrieves.

- India was placing more value on the retrieve in her mouth than her partnership with Ashleigh.

So we went back to doing some recall and 'in-bound' work. Not only was it this that was letting her down, it was also the least arousing part of the retrieve. Bringing the arousal level down in this way meant India was not so engaged with the retrieve item, and she was able to maintain a calmer state. We helped India stay more focused on Ashley during the recalls, and added in difficulty and distraction to proof this behaviour. We also introduced a high value reward (access to a play ball) for a great return, which India loved.

When we went back to retrieves, we made them more difficult, so India didn't have time to concentrate on the dummy as she was using her brain more to overcome the difficulties on the way to and from the retrieve. Incorporating obstacles into the retrieve was a big help, and gave Ashley the opportunity to praise India for getting her returns right.

I also helped Ashley to become more aware of the early signs of over-arousal whilst retrieving (such as being pushy at heel, panting, hovering or paddling her feet), so she could work to reduce and eventually eliminate these to give her more opportunity for success.

contact. If you can't move away, then drop your gaze or turn your shoulder a little, so the dog can come into you. And don't be in a hurry to take the dummy from the dog either.

Possessiveness, Over-Investment in the Retrieve Article

Sometimes when you watch a dog returning with the dummy, you will notice a distinct change in their attention and focus. They may pick the dummy and come halfway back with purpose, but then you start to see them change their focus from wanting to return to their handler to being more interested in the item they have in their mouth, and they start to play with it or mouth it, or just prolong the time they get to hold it by deviating on their return. Some dogs will even stop to urinate on the return, prolonging the time they get to hold on to the dummy.

All this demonstrates the handler's lack of importance in the dog's eyes in the equation: the dog is thinking about the dummy and how nice it is, rather than concentrating on returning and delivering. This is a manifestation of a weakness in recall, as is 'hunting on' (described above) with a dummy in the mouth. When a dog picks the retrieve, its next thought should be 'must get back to handler', not 'what else is out here?' or 'how can I prolong the pleasure in keeping this dummy?'. Again, more work on recalls is required. When you reintroduce the dummy, watch the pick-up closely so that you can praise the dog if he picks and quickly starts to return to you. Also, continue to praise the dog if he is speeding back to you. If he goes to deviate after picking, or hunts on, then use your vocal interruptor immediately to mark this undesirable behaviour – then as soon as the dog changes to come back to you, praise him. Timing is critical here to ensure you don't end up inadvertently rewarding, with praise, any behaviour that you don't want.

Above all, if your dog engages in keeping away, it is imperative not to chase him. The worst thing a handler can do is try and chase after or catch the dog that is staying away or parading around with the retrieve, as this then becomes an even more inter-

A partridge is an ideal size for a young dog's first introduction to picking birds.

esting game of 'chase'. Also, try not to snatch at the dummy, as this will make the dog want to possess its prize even more. Instead, employ some negative psychology and turn away from the dog each time he comes towards you: turn your back on him and move away, and gradually your dog will realise he is getting no attention for his behaviour and will want to reconnect with you.

If your dog is doing this in a group situation, ask the other members of the group to ensure their dogs are secure at heel so they don't join in the game, and also ask them to kindly ignore your dog if he approaches them trying to get their attention. You need to cut down the rewards that the dog is receiving from its environment and actions. The first step, however, is to backtrack and work on this behaviour alone, in a less distracting environment.

Delivery of Game

Retrieving canvas or plastic dummies is one thing, but making the transition to retrieving game can be another thing altogether. Sometimes dogs will start to mouth or mess around with game. This may be due to the unfamiliar texture or feel of feathers (or fur) in their mouth, or to the unusual weight distribution. This is usually rectified with plenty of exposure and practice.

Before taking a dog out into the shooting field for the first time, it is advisable to give it some experience of picking cold game first. If you can acquire some partridge these are ideal in that they are small with tight feathers. Don't be tempted to use woodpigeon as they have very loose feathers and can be difficult for a young dog. If the dog is picking partridge cleanly, then you can progress to other birds such as pheasant, duck or grouse, if you are lucky enough to get any. Next, let your dog have a warm bird after a drive, and progress from there.

Putting birds down and nosing at them is just due to unfamiliarity, and will usually cease with more exposure to retrieving game. If you can let the dog go sweeping after a drive and let it pick birds quickly, deliver to you and then be sent straight off again to hunt for more, you should find that your dog gets more used to handling and delivering game.

Possession and 'Hanging On'

Some dogs bring in a retrieve and want to hold on to their prize, so will put their head down, arching their neck, rather than raising their head up to deliver to hand. If you notice this, try to isolate this behaviour indoors by putting the retrieve item down on the floor and getting your dog to pick it up and then focus on you. Be patient and vocally praise the dog when it looks up at you. Then use a food reward (or toy) to reward the dog when it raises its head up to your hand to deliver. Do not reward any 'head down' deliveries. If you are consistent, you will be able to reset a 'head up' delivery pattern.

Dogs that hang on to game rather than delivering it tenderly to hand often do so as a result of excitement or stress, and not just possession. Many seasoned gundogs will readily release their quarry to hand on a shoot day, out picking up, but are more reluctant to give up their retrieve at a field trial. It appears that the added pressure and stress under these conditions have a role to play here. Whether this emanates from the handler or is something that is picked up from the competition of all the other dogs is uncertain, but it is

Competition conditions may cause pressure, which in turn can affect the way a dog delivers its retrieve.

Rosie, a five-year-old Labrador, had an in-grained habit of wanting to hold on to her retrieve for as long as possible, and Janet was unsure of how she could rectify this issue. This pattern had been going on for several years, so was not something that was going to be resolved overnight. But with patience and consistency, Janet was able to achieve some improvement by helping her dog understand what she was looking for in terms of a delivery to hand.

Rosie was coming back to her quickly, which was good, but she was keeping the bird to herself, wanting to hold on to it for longer. She would rather keep her prize, and knew that Janet would just take it away from her. So we worked to change her mindset so that she wanted to offer Janet the bird in return for a reward that she wanted.

Working indoors from a static position, I recommended the use of a clicker and food rewards to shape a nice 'head up' delivery. This allowed precise marking of the required behaviour. Janet had to become quite adept at her timing of praise and reward, otherwise Rosie would inadvertently be encouraged to 'spit out' the dummy in anticipation of receiving the treat. This was not something that Janet had tried before, and it does require somebody who can help with the process, so that it is clear for the dog.

Another thing we talked through before returning to the field was the idea that we were looking for Rosie to 'give' Janet the retrieve, rather than her 'taking' it, so that she would avoid snatching at the dummy, rushing or bending forwards over her. A little 'reverse' psychology went a long way here. Getting Janet to put her hands behind her back as Rosie approached was a great way to remind her not to grab at the dummy, and it led to Rosie trying to push the retrieve towards Janet instead.

Putting your hands behind your back as your dog returns is a good way to stop you from grabbing at the dummy.

a behaviour that is commonly seen. A bird that is still flapping will often be held more tightly by the dog and can also provoke this 'hanging on' response.

To alleviate any handler pressure, try to be as relaxed as possible when the dog comes in towards you, and do not stare directly at the dog, as this can add pressure. Drop your gaze from the dog, or even turn your shoulder away a little, and let the dog come in towards you without reaching too quickly for the bird. Allow the dog time to come in and present its quarry. At this point, praise the dog before giving it your release cue.

Avoid face-to-face contact on delivery by letting the dog follow you at heel with the dummy when it returns.

If you have a dog that has demonstrated this behaviour under competition conditions several times, there is little point in continuing to compete with the dog, where it will just be repeating the behaviour. It would be better to remove the dog from those situations, and take it out picking up, where you can go back to rehearsing the sort of deliveries that you do want, thus resetting a pattern of desired behaviour.

Dropping or Spitting Out Retrieves

Dropping or spitting out a retrieve is not a common problem with most well-bred gundogs, who will usually carry things around seemingly just for the pleasure of doing so. As with any issue, it is important to understand why the dog is spitting out the retrieve or dropping it. There can be various reasons for this. The dog may perceive the retrieve to have no value, or rather there is no value in it continuing to hold the retrieve. The dog may be finding other things in its environment more rewarding, such as ground scent, other dogs/people, or

the desire to continue hunting, or it may be in a rush to go and get the next retrieve (particularly in a picking-up situation, where there are multiple birds down). In other cases the issue may be handler induced, whereby food has been used, with poor timing, to improve deliv-

Positive body contact and praise while the dog holds the dummy. The handler doesn't take the dummy away immediately.

ery, and the dog is spitting out the dummy in anticipation of receiving the food.

To resolve this issue it is important to rebuild value into the dog retaining the retrieve, through praise and positive body contact. When the dog approaches you with the item, make no attempt to take it or snatch at it. First, start to move away from the dog as he comes near, rather than standing still and letting him drop it at your feet. This will mean that, rather than stopping and dropping, the dog will have to make the effort to keep coming towards you, and this will give you an opportunity to praise him for continuing to hold on to the dummy.

In addition, rather than facing the dog, which can be off-putting for some dogs, you can turn so that the dog is following you and coming up into a heel position. You can now let the dog walk along beside you at heel with the retrieve in his mouth. Remember to praise him so that he knows this is a desired behaviour, and then when you are ready, take the retrieve out of the dog's mouth as you walk along.

If the dog is happy to face you, head on, when he returns, let him come past you or just into your vicinity, and then try to put your hands on the dog's body to give him some positive body contact and praise through touch and stroking while the dog is retaining his hold on the retrieve. If the dog drops the retrieve, cease the body contact and praise, and turn away from the dog. Give him the opportunity to pick the retrieve up again, and if he does so, recommence the praise and body fussing routine. He will soon begin to understand that holding on to the retrieve leads to reward and attention.

DELIVERY FROM WATER

A common issue when retrieving on or over water is the dog dropping the dummy to shake on its return. Long-coated dogs are particularly prone to shake in order to relieve the heaviness of water in their coats. But most dogs will want to shake once they have got wet. Whilst shaking is not an issue if the dog maintains his hold on the bird, there is the increased risk that in so doing he may accidentally let go of the bird. In extreme cases, the dog puts down or drops the bird to shake, before attempting to pick it up again and return to the handler.

CASE STUDY: STAR'S SLOW RETURNS FROM WATER

Ian had successfully resolved the issue he was having with his three-year-old dog Star dropping the dummy after she came out of water, and he was pleased that she was now maintaining her hold. But despite being a fast dog and a strong swimmer, whenever she got out of the water, she would come back almost at a crawl in a very slow-motion manner towards him, with no pace or enthusiasm. He didn't understand why she was doing this.

I asked him how he had taught her not to drop, and he told me that he had been encouraging her out of water and then shouting 'hold, hold' as she came towards him to reinforce her holding on to the dummy. I asked him whether he did this behaviour when she was retrieving normally from land, and of course he replied 'no'. He was treating the two retrieve scenarios quite differently, and what he hadn't realised was that this different behaviour was inadvertently putting a lot of pressure on Star. She was already holding the dummy, so couldn't do much more than that, and therefore she was not sure whether she was getting the exercise right or wrong. Once Ian recognised this he was quickly able to rectify the situation by praising her instead when she was holding the dummy, so she had the positive feedback that she needed and understood that she was doing the right thing. Fairly soon she was flying back towards him again, both on water and land.

Praise the dog while it retains its hold on the dummy in the water.

Take the dummy just as the dog leaves the water, so there is no time for him to drop it or shake himself.

Gradually you will be able to increase your distance from the water's edge.

Shaking can also give you an indication of the dog's attitude, in that those dogs that shake are sometimes thinking of their own comfort, rather than being focused on their task. You can liken this to a human coming out of the sea after a pleasure swim and grabbing for a towel to wrap around themselves to keep warm, whereas the serious triathlete swimmer will keep moving forwards to get to the bicycle, focusing on the next part of their challenge.

Understandably then, for working gundogs, removing shaking from the equation is usually seen as desirable, and many handlers will seek to put this on cue before doing much serious water work.

Before working on delivery out of water, you should ensure that your deliveries on land are solid. There is no point in introducing the additional degree of difficulty of maintaining a hold coming out of water, if the dog has not fully grasped the concept under normal field conditions.

The following two methods are very effective in helping the dog understand what you require.

Method 1: Stay Close to the Dog

Ideally, find a stretch of water with a gently sloping beach entry, where you can get into the water with the dog. Throw your retrieve out into the deeper water, and as your dog returns to you carrying the retrieve, praise him for successfully holding the retrieve and not dropping it. If you only have access to a steeper-sided pond, get right up to and almost into the water, and as your dog comes to the edge but is still in the water, praise him for maintaining the hold and then actively take the retrieve out of his mouth before he has any time to try to get out of the water or to drop it. You are trying to set up a pattern of your dog getting it right – that is, not dropping the dummy and being rewarded for holding it.

As the dog becomes consistent at this then you will gradually start to move a little further away. The next step will be that the dog is just starting to come out of the water as you take the dummy. Remember to keep praising the dog all the while it is maintaining the hold and not dropping, and then just take the dummy using your release cue 'dead'. If the dog drops it, then backtrack so you are getting a few more right again, before once again moving on.

Soon the dog will be coming up on to the bank, and beyond, and you will still be praising him for maintaining his hold on the dummy. He will have learnt through repetition what is required.

Method 2: Run Away from the Dog

This method relies on your dog's chase instinct. Use the same method of praising the dog for swimming holding the dummy, and then as he starts to come out of the water, turn away from him (rather than standing there to receive the dummy) and start running away. Keep your back to your dog so he has to chase after you to catch up with you. Doing this overrides the dog's concentration on the retrieve and relieving his coat, as he is more concerned with keeping up with you as you move away.

You can then let the dog catch up with you at heel. Then, as you are walking along, take the dummy with your release cue.

Above and opposite, top: As the dog starts to come out of the water, run away so he has to catch up with you.

DAMAGING GAME AND 'HARD MOUTH'

There is a strong stigma attached to damaging game and 'hard mouth' in a gundog, and with good reason, because birds that are damaged when retrieving are deemed not fit for the table. The trait of being 'hard mouthed' is an eliminating fault in a field trial, so it is something to be avoided. There is a strong belief that this is an inherited trait, and to a degree this may have been true, particularly in some of the imported HPR lines, where mouth may not have been actively selected for when breeding. However, you often see well-bred retrievers with different pedigree lines but the same handler, and they appear to have 'mouth issues,' or rather issues that result in problems with mouth and delivery.

So it is necessary to look at why dogs damage game, and to try to avoid some of the instances that may lead to it. It is probably not possible to train dogs not to damage game, but it is certainly possible to provoke them to do so, or make conditions more probable for them to do it.

As Susan Scales says in her book *Retriever Training* (1992): 'There is no real cure for hard mouth, although I have heard it said that taking the dog to

Feel from the back, across the ribs to check a bird for damage. The ribs should be barrel shaped.

a really big covert shoot and giving him bird after bird may do the trick.' She also goes on to say that 'hard mouth is very rare in genuine working strains of retriever, unless the dog has been made so by mistakes in training.'

Thankfully, selective breeding over many generations of retrievers has given us dogs with soft mouths. So what are some of the common mistakes made in training that could lead to issues with mouth?

Why Dogs Damage Game

Rushing a young dog into the field and then sending him for a strong runner before he is used to picking lots of game carefully can lead to problems further down the line. Ideally you should make the transition from picking warm dead game to picking a live bird very carefully. Selecting a partridge or small hen bird that has a little life in it and that can be picked out of light cover calmly under quiet supervision is a much better choice than sending your young dog for an old, wily cock bird in front of an audience of expectant guns.

If a dog is spurred by a cock bird – it might rake its sharp spurs across the dog's eyes or mouth – this can be a certain way of causing a dog to give it a squeeze to stop this problem occurring in the future. The dog has then found a successful way of dealing with a problematic and painful experience.

Other birds that you should take extreme caution with picking are coots, which have feet with exceptionally sharp talons. Also, do not send your dog for corvids (such as magpies or crows), which, if not

An inexperienced dog picking a lively cock bird runner may end up getting spurred.

dead, can give your dog an aggressive peck with their sharp beaks.

Another major factor in dogs damaging birds, and probably the main cause in well-bred sensitive dogs, is that they respond to perceived pressure from their owner, or they feel anxious coming back to a large line of people, particularly in a competition situation.

Also, if your dog has played 'keep away' with a retrieve before and you have told it off for doing something on its way back to you, then again, the dog may feel anxious. Sometimes this can cause it to start mouthing or biting down on the retrieve in its mouth as it returns.

If you have any sort of recall, return or delivery issues with your dog, as mentioned earlier in the chapter, it is best to do some remedial work on these first without a dummy in the dog's mouth at all. This

A wounded corvid can peck a dog aggressively.

takes the retrieve article out of the equation, so you can work on polishing the return and present to front. Correcting a dog with a dummy in its mouth is never a good idea.

What is Dog Damage?

Dogs usually damage game by crushing the ribcage in on both sides, often squeezing it or crunching it. If you feel the ribcage of a bird and it is 'in' on one side only, then this may not be down to dog damage, but rather damage that has occurred through being close shot, or shot with a heavy load.

In a trial, if a judge has not seen where the dog picked the bird from, and it comes back damaged, it is very hard for them to make a true assessment. It may be that the dog had to drag a live bird through some stock fencing to reach it, or it fell on a rocky slope, which led to the damage. In either of these instances, it won't have been a hard mouth that has caused the damage, and the dog should be given the benefit of the doubt.

Usually it is very obvious when a dog damages game as you can see it, and often hear it, as the dog returns to its handler.

7 HANDLING ISSUES

*Together — one of the most inspiring words
in the English language. Coming together is a
beginning; keeping together is progress; working
together is success.*

EDWARD EVERETT HALE

LINING ISSUES

Having a dog that will run out in a straight line from
your side to a given area is a great asset in achieving an efficient retrieve of an unmarked bird. But this
skill is something that can take a long time to perfect.
It is built through nurturing the dog's trust in your
cues and maintaining consistency. If the foundation
work for sending on blind retrieves has not been carried out methodically and at an appropriate pace for
the dog, this will lead to problems in the dog's confidence on the send-away and outrun.

No-Gos and 'Popping'

The dog that refuses to be sent on a true blind, or
goes so far then stops or 'pops', can be very frustrating. Many trainers will have come across this problem, and it is nearly always because of a lack of confidence on the dog's part. Quite often the trainer has
progressed too quickly, trying to push the dog on to
true blinds before it is capable, and therefore the dog
hasn't gained total trust or belief in the cues for the
blind send-away. This results in a build-up of anxiety
in the dog, which can lead to a refusal to go (sometimes termed 'stickiness'), lip licking and sideways
glances at the handler. The dog feels unable to move
off as it is unsure of what it is being asked to do.

In other cases, trainers have relied too much on
single specific cues for blind retrieves. For example,
saluting the area with a shot, so that the dog always
relates the shot to a retrieve being there, but if there is
no shot then they won't go; or using a white dummy
or visual marker to line towards using sight. Again,
if this visual cue is removed the dog doesn't understand the exercise.

It is important to review your cues for blind
retrieves to understand not only what you think they
are, but also what the dog understands. For example,
they could include (but should not be restricted to)

Make the chances of success greater with visual
dummies or markers to build a confident habit
of running.

When I got Twig at sixteen months, she didn't have any real concept of running a line to a blind retrieve. Her outrun was unreliable to memory blinds, and she was highly environmentally distracted. I had to build her belief in my hand cues, so they meant 'run' in the first instance, and then only later on would I be able to fine tune direction. Because she didn't have a solid foundation of cues for blind retrieves, she was prone to not going at all, or stuttering and stopping.

This was very much our weakest area, and I spent months working exclusively on this. Because she was already quite old, the temptation was to rush because she should have been further on than she was. I tried a two-pronged approach when I was lining her out: first, I was aiming to build from scratch positively to get her running, but if she did deviate off course to investigate things that were distracting her I let her go, as long as there was no way for her to self-reward by finding another retrieve.

In the time that I worked on this we didn't really work on much else. I kept things as simple as possible with the intention of building a good muscle memory with every single successful retrieve. With this in mind, I set myself a '100 strong lines challenge'. This meant achieving outruns to memory blinds without hesitation, or any head wobbling, or looking over her shoulder as she went. These 'lines' were extremely simple, to short visual dummies at just twenty yards, or to longer trailing memory blinds, or longer visual targets or memory areas. I made sure I mixed up the use of non-visual memory areas with the occasional visual targets, as I didn't want over-reliance on a visual stimulus. Twig is very motivated by sight, and also by shot sound, so it was important to build her outrun habit without these two elements.

Each time I took Twig out to do this outrun practice, we only did five or six retrieves in one session, and I graded these outruns as follows:

- Green: total success, with Twig powering out to the retrieve confidently.
- Amber: a certain amount of looking over her shoulder or wobbling, but keeping going.
- Yellow: running strongly, but not in the right direction.
- Red: total failure of the exercise.

To ensure I kept things simple, I was aiming for a 95 per cent green success rate.

I also used a handling collar on her for the majority of the time, so that she was in the right position – in fact she could maintain this without the collar, but I wanted to be able to feel her pulling to run when she heard my verbal send cue – I wanted to know that she was keen to run.

shot, visible dummy, visual marker post, hand signal, arm movement, pushing your cap up, voice, retracing your steps, putting on a handling collar, familiar ground, a comfort area where retrieves are normally placed, and training alone.

From this list of cues, ensure that the personal set-up cues (such as your body movements, voice and so on) remain consistent. Then be aware of the environmental cues that you and the dog are using, and try to vary them, or not be over-reliant on a single one. By all means use a visual target to run the dog to, but also start work on being able to fade this visual aspect, and do other memory blinds without a visual element, but using another cue (such as footfall, for example) instead.

If you are experiencing some of these anxiety issues with your dog, it is important to simplify and go back to doing some building work on simple lines, but also try

Using a handling collar to maintain Twig in the correct heel position to send for a blind retrieve.

At the 100 retrieve goal, I was pleased to have achieved 96 green, three amber and one yellow, with no reds. In the following set of 100 retrieves, this average dropped off considerably as I started to introduce a greater degree of difficulty as Twig became more confident. She was now running, but not taking a very good line. This stemmed from her not relating to my arm and hand set-up very well at all – she wasn't using this cue to relate to direction: it merely meant 'go' to her now. Eventually I had to adapt my hand signal so it started lower down, and this enabled her to pick up the hand in her sight line more readily and use it to reference where she should be going.

to remember to reinforce each cue in the chain. You can do this using a clicker and treat, or vocally praising the dog as it achieves confidence in the cues. For example, if you send the dog and it doesn't go, or you call it back for stopping and then you try again, you have rehearsed one failure. If the dog doesn't go again or goes wrong a third time, your percentage success rate is dropping and dropping. Now, out of four attempts you only have a 25 per cent success rate, and this isn't enough for the dog to build on. You should really be aiming for at least a 90 per cent success rate, so that the dog has a lot of muscle-memory practice of getting it right, with only the occasional 'wrong'.

Going the Second Time

Quite often handlers will remark that they have a dog that doesn't go first time when it is sent on a blind retrieve, but when they send it for a second time it goes out perfectly well. They will ask how to deal with this issue, and I have a 100 per cent reliable method to suggest to them that never fails to solve the issue: don't send the dog twice!

The dog has learned a pattern of behaviour and you need to break this cycle. To do this, simplify your practice memory blind retrieves to such an extent that the dog will not fail to go. This may mean using a very visual dummy on bare ground, or making the retrieve exceptionally short. You want to reset a new pattern of always going the first time.

If you do get a no-go, then break away from that exercise. Do not be tempted to resend as you will just be starting the undesired pattern of behaviour again. Do something else with the dog that it can do, such as a marked retrieve or some heelwork, and then go back and reset the exercise into an easier format that will be achievable for the dog.

Taking a Poor Line

If your dog has not fully learned the blind cues, it will still tend to think for itself where it should be going. This means that it may veer towards the fall of previous marked retrieves, or towards a gun, or go off course due to terrain, wind or cover changes (*see* below for lining through cover). Therefore, once the dog is confident in the concept of running blinds, it is time to concentrate on ensuring that the line to the retrieve is accurate. A poor line out will mean that the trainer has to step in and start handling to keep the dog on course to retrieve, and this makes the overall retrieve much less efficient.

There are two different strategies for addressing line deviations.

Stay there and try again: When the dog deviates from the line, call it back and start again. Give it the same information in the same place and let it go again. Watch what it does. You are looking for the dog to adapt its behaviour as the first attempt has been unsuccessful. You might have to try this three or four times, and the dog may offer other variations of behaviour that are not what you want. Ensure that you don't change any of your cues for the send-away, so that the dog is given consistent input from you each time, and then he can try to change his behaviour to get a more successful outcome. If, after four attempts, the dog is still not maintaining the line that you want, then you will need to look at shortening or simplifying the exercise.

Moving forwards on the line: When the dog deviates from the line, stop it, walk out to it and bring it back on to the correct line; then resend it from there. This way you are reinforcing the line. You might have to do this a couple of times, depending on the length of the retrieve, before the dog hits the target. You can then reset the exercise and repeat to reinforce the desired line.

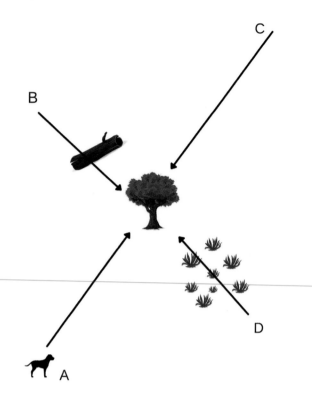

'Comfort area' exercise.

If a dog veers off course, reset it so it can take the correct line, rather than handling on.

DRILLS TO IMPROVE CONFIDENCE

Using a Comfort Area

This exercise builds confidence in blinds with young dogs. It is a progression from straightforward single 'trailing memory blinds'. It uses a visual area where the dog has picked from before, as a 'comfort area' to keep running back to. The purpose is to develop your dog's skills in continuing to hold a line, and for the dog to gain confidence in the blind send-away/set-up.

Use a tree, cone or stake, or any strong visual reference point as a marker to place out four or five dummies. You can take the dog with you to place the dummies, or leave it at a distance from where you will make the first retrieve.

You can adapt the distance from the comfort area to suit both the stage of the dog and the terrain you are working in. For example, you might want to do your first retrieve starting from A at 50 metres away, and then walk round to a different location to

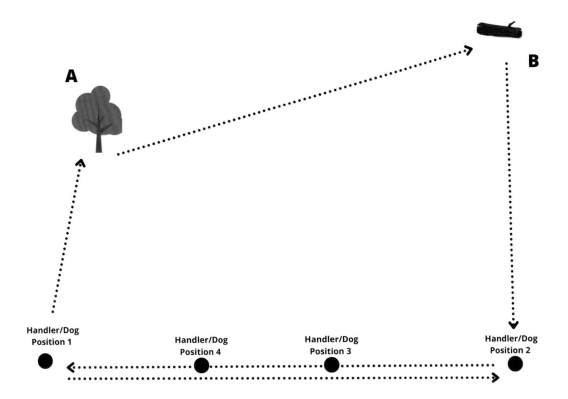

A

B

Handler/Dog
Position 1

Handler/Dog
Position 4

Handler/Dog
Position 3

Handler/Dog
Position 2

'Two's comfy' exercise.

send back to your area, but this time your line may incorporate some thicker cover or an obstacle, so you decide to shorten your distance to 30 metres to achieve success. On the next send you may lengthen the distance again, and so on.

You will be walking in a loose circle around the comfort area and sending back to it from different locations. You don't have to pick all the dummies that you put down. If you achieve what you want (confident straight lines to the area) then finish on that. You can always revisit the exercise in a different format another day. If the dog struggles at all, then you need to simplify, either by shortening your lines or 'walking the line', or by re-marking the area with dummies.

Advancing the Comfort Area

This is a progressive exercise, following on from the drill described above. Whereas the previous set-up employed a single familiar area, this drill uses two separate areas. You can use this exercise to continue building confi-

dence in memory blinds. It uses two strong visual areas where the dog has picked from before.

The purpose of the exercise is to develop your dog's skills in continuing to hold a line and for the dog to gain confidence in the blind send-away and set-up cues.

Starting at handler/dog position 1, walk with the dog to visual area A and leave two large drill dummies. Then walk on with the dog to visual area B and leave two more large drill dummies, before walking to handler/dog position 2. From here you will turn round and line the dog straight back to area B to pick one dummy.

Next, walk on to handler/dog position 3 and line the dog from here to pick one of the dummies from area A. Then walk on to handler/dog position 4, and line the dog from here to pick the remaining dummy from area B. Finally, walk back to handler/dog position 1, and line the dog from here to pick the last dummy at area A.

Variation

You can then repeat this drill, but this time leave the dog at handler/dog position 1, whilst you walk to A and B and back along the previous lines. Then you will do the retrieves in reverse order, so sending the dog from position 1 to pick from A; from position 4 to pick at B; from position 3 to pick at A; and finally from position 2 to pick at B.

WORKING THROUGH COVER

Whilst your early retrieve work with a young dog is invariably done on bare grass so that the dummies remain very visual, there will come a time when you will want to teach the dog about going into or through cover. And you will want them to do this confidently and without hesitation. As with any unusual aspect of new terrain (natural or man-made), your introduction should be done in a sensitive manner so that you nurture confidence in the new environment. Being over-eager to force a young dog into dense cover for no reason can actually be detrimental and serve to put them off altogether if you are not careful. For example, thick brambles can be particularly challenging, and young nettles that are coming up in the spring will be very sharp and may cause rashes and a lot of discomfort from contact, both at the time and for a long time afterwards. So, pick your first introduction to cover thoughtfully, and manage how you are going to work with this new feature. Some thicker long grass or reeds is enough for a first introduction

Stand in the cover and send the dog out for the retrieve so that he cannot skirt round it.

for a young dog. This can be consolidated later with more challenging cover, once confidence and enthusiasm are established.

Cover Shy?

If you find that your young dog seems rather cover shy then you need to give him a good reason to investigate cover. A keen retriever can usually be enticed to investigate with a marked retrieve of a dummy thrown into light cover, or likewise a spaniel can be enticed to hunt in pockets of cover to find a tennis ball. Once they are tackling that keenly then you can try and throw the dummy or ball a bit deeper into thicker cover.

Another tactic is to let a young puppy chase round after an older dog into areas of slightly thicker cover. The larger dog will blaze a trail and the youngster will be keen to follow if the activity looks fun. With this method, there is no retrieve involved – the pup is just following another dog. You may be able to set this up with one of your (or someone else's) older, more experienced dogs that will happily lead the way into thicker cover, hunting or investigating smells.

A later step will be getting the youngster to cross or go through a patch of cover that might be forming an obstacle or barrier. The temptation in this case will

A spaniel enjoys hunting some cover to find a ball.

be for the pup to scoot round it, picking an easy path. Rather than trying to force a young pup to face cover in this respect, both on the way to and from a retrieve, which may be too much of a big ask, try stepping into the cover with the dog yourself and then sending the dog out of the cover for the retrieve. This way the pup is tackling the cover in a positive manner, and there is no option, if the dog wants the retrieve, not to negotiate the cover to get there. This will prevent any habit of 'running round' from occurring. And the excitement of the retrieve should help draw the youngster through what it perceives as tricky cover.

Finally, once your dog has discovered the joys of cover – and in later life it will soon learn that this is where the birds tend to be found, tucked up – you need to ensure that he will also leave cover when requested. Young dogs may find breaking out of longer grass to go on to bare terrain challenging, as they see this as a barrier, and are used to finding their dummies hidden in this grass. With this in mind, don't throw all your retrieves into cover, but make certain that you practise working your dog on barer ground outside areas of cover. For example, with a more experienced dog, practise hunt exercises on bare stubble or drill in front of field margins or headland. Or after completing some retrieves in a sugar-beet field or cover crop remember to do some retrieves that fall outside this cover and on to a track or area that doesn't have cover.

Holding a Line

Whilst most gundogs will often naturally gravitate towards cover when they are hunting, it seems that some, and particularly retrievers when they are running out to a retrieve, will do everything they can to avoid running through it. It makes sense, however, to pick the path of least resistance, particularly if you are travelling at speed, and just like humans, many dogs will 'path follow' or pick an easy route that avoids difficult obstacles or cover. For instance, you would not want to wade through chest-high bracken if you could find an easy sheep track on the side of a moorland hill

Taking a path provides an easier option than pushing through cover, but this may take the dog off course for the retrieve.

Karen's dog Bob was a powerful retriever with plenty of desire, but he was very prone to pick the easiest route to a retrieve, not staying on line through areas of cover. Karen wanted to improve on this as it was affecting the efficiency of the retrieve, and sometimes meant that the dog was taking significant detours where it could disturb game.

We set up some retrieves and exercises specifically with this in mind, but in a simplified way, whilst we helped Bob to understand what was required.

Using Marked Retrieves

We used thrown dummies and sent immediately, rather than using blinds, to give Bob more desire and impetus to power through the cover to reach his target. Once we had achieved success, and proofed it, we were then able to move on to using delayed marks incorporating varying cover.

Walking the Line

Next, we built the line to memory blinds by taking Bob with us to place the dummy and then walking back with him along the exact line we wanted him to take. This meant going through the cover together and crossing any obstacles in our path, so he was familiar with them. This helped to confirm the concept for Bob, making it easy for him to succeed. For longer retrieves, we broke this line down into segments. This meant we placed three dummies in the area, walked about one-third of the way away from it through the cover, and sent him back. Then we moved back along the line through the cover again and repeated from two-thirds of the distance, before repeating one more time from the full distance. This really helped to establish the dog's confidence in the line as he was repeating the last section.

Recalls before Retrieves

On other retrieves, we left Bob remotely where we would later leave the dummy and walked back away from him and then called him to us, ensuring that he took the same

---

– it just makes life a lot easier! So it is hard to blame your dog for wanting to take an easier route. However, sometimes doing this can throw them off course, and detracts from what would be a straightforward mark if they had held the line despite the terrain. In turn, this may mean having to handle the dog that has deviated too far off course. With this in mind, it is worth taking the time and effort to teach your dog to hold its line straight through cover or over obstacles.

CASTING PROBLEMS

The common issues that are seen with casting (left, right and back) usually fall into two categories: not taking a strong cast, and taking an incorrect cast.

Not Taking a Strong Cast

If the dog doesn't take a strong cast he may be moving only a few metres before he stops again to ask for more input, or he may go in the general direction of the cast but without pace, or hunting as he goes. For this issue, as with poor lining, more work needs to be done on instilling confidence in the cast, and reinforcing that it means run in that direction rather than hunt. To establish a run habit, set the dog up to do some static casts remotely from you, and use visual dummies that are direct marks or memories placed a long way out from the dog (for example, 20 to 30 metres). This will help the dog understand that it needs to run when given the cast.

direct line through the cover that we had walked through. From there, we repeated the exercise, but this time left the dummy out a short distance behind Bob; we recalled him to us, and then Karen sent him from her side all the way back to the known dummy on the line that he had already recalled on.

Start in Cover and Move Out

As well as expecting Bob to run a line, go through the cover and out and maintain his line, we did some exercises where we started by standing in the cover and throwing a mark on to the clear ground beyond. Then we did this exercise as a memory blind, with a visual white dummy that Bob could see from his position in the cover. This way Bob had to get out of the cover to pick, and then come back into the cover to return, so any thought of running around the cover was eliminated. Later we were able to back chain this exercise so that we started further away from the retrieve but just outside the cover, gradually building the line.

This dog has taken the directional cast but is hunting towards the retrieve, rather than running.

The dog has acted on his own initiative in pulling back, instead of taking on board the cue given by the handler to go left.

Taking an Incorrect Cast

This usually happens because the dog is guessing what the handler wants, or he already has an idea where he might be going, rather than actually going where he is directed. In this case it is useful to use some differentiation to help the dog understand where he should be going.

The walking baseball exercise, whereby you set the dog up remotely again and use two dummies for different casts, is a fun way of reinforcing your casting.

Walking Baseball Exercise

Take the dog to some bare ground. Sit him up and throw one dummy over his head, which would be a 'back' cast, and then another out squarely to the right, which will be a 'right' cast. This exercise works best with a dog that already has a good understanding of left, right and back casts, as you will be sending the dog for the first dummy thrown rather than the last.

Once you have picked that, you can reposition the dog so that you can use the other dummy for a cast of your choice, but first throwing the other dummy out in a different direction. This exercise helps the dog learn to watch you closely, as it knows there are two dummies available but it needs to take direction from you to pick the correct one.

You can vary how you use this exercise. When

Short casts to marked retrieves on a walking baseball exercise help to support the dog's understanding of directional casting.

you start off, you might want to send the dog for the second dummy thrown to ensure a high degree of success and to establish confidence. Then, later, you can swap to sending for the first one thrown. You can also use the exercise to reinforce a particular cast. For example, one day just work on always pushing 'back' for the dummy that is behind the dog, then another day do random casts so that the dog cannot predict a pattern. This is a fun way for improving confidence and commitment.

Try to restrict the number of retrieves you do from this exercise to about six or seven in one session so that you do not overload the dog and bore it.

Stop-Clock Drill

This drill is a progression of the walking baseball drill in that you incorporate send-aways and stops as well into the exercise.

Prior to running this drill, using a clock face, pre-plant one large visual dummy at 3 o'clock and one at 9 o'clock. Then bring your dog out and leave him at the centre of the clock while you walk out and throw two dummies to 12 o'clock. Then pick up one of these dummies.

Next walk back with your dog to 6 o'clock. You are now going to line your dog towards 12 o'clock and let him pick the dummy there. When he returns, set him

up and send him away again towards 12 o'clock, but this time you will stop him in the centre of the clock. You are now going to cast him right to 3 o'clock. If he does not take the cast and pulls back, you can allow him to do so as he cannot self-reward as there is no dummy at 12 o'clock. When he has satisfied himself

Lining up to pick the dummy at 12 o'clock.

Casting the dog to pick the dummy at 3 o'clock.

that there is no dummy to be found in that area you can either recall him, stop him again at the centre and recast, or go out and collect him and place him back at the centre of the clock before recasting.

When you have successfully cast to 3 o'clock, let the dog see you drop the dummy where you are standing at 6 o'clock, and walk back through the centre together. Now turn round and send the dog back to 6 o'clock to pick this dummy. When he returns, you can resend him, stopping him in the centre. You will then once more cast him right-handed for the remaining pre-planted dummy.

Again, you can vary this exercise so that you pre-plant the two casting dummies in one area instead of putting them in different areas (for example, both at 3 o'clock). This will give your dog more confidence as it will have successfully picked from that area already.

Author's note: I ran this drill with two of my novice dogs, and they both had very different approaches. Brae was hard-charging with strong outruns to the long back dummy, stopping well, but not taking on board the directional information I gave him the first

time round. He assumed he knew what he was doing, and instead of casting right as directed, he ignored the cast and went back to where he thought the dummy would be. This showed that he still trusted his own instinct over my information. I repeated this exercise without any vocal correction, so he went down to the back dummy area and checked this out to find nothing there. He then took my cast on the third time, realising that I had valuable information to give him.

Twig approached this differently. Her head was flicking towards the right-hand cast area from the outset. She had noticed this dummy and I could tell that she was already thinking about it. Her outrun had less power and certainty, and when she stopped she was already swinging round to the right. Therefore she was willing to take the right-hand cast as she wasn't fully committed to the back dummy area. Each time she stopped and took the cast without pulling back. I thought she would find the pull of the back dummy irresistible, as Brae had done, but she was actually one step ahead of me in overthinking on this exercise.

This exercise reinforced some learning about these individual dogs and their styles, and also reminds us that these exercises need to be tailored or modified to meet the needs of different dogs. For example, the next time I ran this exercise with Twig I ensured that the pre-planted casting dummy was not so obvious. I wanted to see if she would still take the cast despite the draw of the back dummy. We achieved success and after that, I didn't repeat this drill with her, as I wanted to return to working on maintaining her outrun.

STOP ISSUES

If your dog's response to the stop whistle is poor – for example it is slow, with the dog taking in more ground than necessary, or it lacks focus on you once it has stopped – then it is time to do something about this issue. Draw a line in the sand and review what is the best stop that your dog is capable of, and look at the conditions that you are achieving this under. For example, it might be on your walk or at home in the garden, with no retrieving involved and under minimally distracting conditions. Your dog might also stop promptly going towards a blind retrieve, but gives a much less sharp response when hunting or working on a marked retrieve. Make a note of all of these instances. The difference in response will be down to your partnership, motivation and reinforcement. Only once you have set some benchmarks can you do anything to improve your stop whistle response.

In terms of style, some dogs spin round and sit up in a very smart fashion. Others turn round and stand in a more fluid manner. Each dog will have his own response type, and you won't be able to completely change that. But it is the attitude and response time that you will be looking to improve upon.

Improving Poor Stops

If the stop whistle has not been taught and conditioned methodically and thoroughly then it is likely that, when you start adding in environmental factors, some weakness will show up and the dog won't stop as you wish. In addition to the whistle not being ful-

Review how your dog is stopping on the whistle, and whether this can be improved.

If the stop whistle is not fully conditioned then the dog may not stop when it is on unfamiliar ground.

With the help of a friend you can set up this exercise, which will help your dog understand that you have valuable input to give in terms of finding the retrieve. Have your assistant go out to an area and pre-plant a dummy (at B), then walk away from it to the side, to a distance of about twenty metres. This dummy should be placed downwind from the thrower.

Next, ask your assistant to throw a marked retrieve for you that lands relatively near them (at A). Allow your dog to mark this dummy and then turn round, with the dog, to face away from it while your assistant picks it back up again. Now, turn back towards the area of the fall and send your dog for this delayed marked retrieve. He should remember where it landed, and will go out and start hunting that area. Watch what he does, and after he has had a short hunt, stop him using your whistle. If he stops promptly, praise him and then cast him to where the pre-planted dummy is so that he gets a further reward for working with you.

If he doesn't stop you have two options: you can leave him to hunt around of his own accord for a while and not find anything. Gradually he will lose belief in his own judgement, and when you see his body language change to more uncertainty, and looking as if he will be more receptive to your input, you can try another stop whistle, and if he stops praise him and carry on with the cast. This method is one of attrition. You ignore his inappropriate response to your cues but keep delivering the same information, which, if he takes it, will help him to succeed.

Alternatively, as soon as he doesn't stop on the whistle you can go out, collect him and reset him in position as described

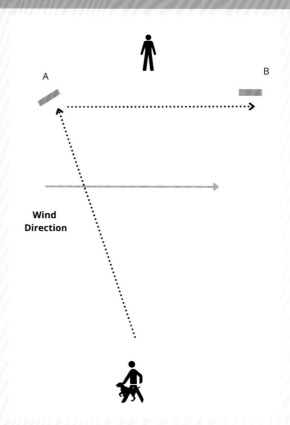

In the moving mark exercise, a helper will throw the mark to A and then remove it, enabling the handler to stop and cast their dog to a new position B.

above, before returning to your place, re-blowing the whistle, praising him and continuing with the cast to the pre-planted dummy.

This is an exercise that can be used occasionally to test how your partnership is working with your dog and his readiness to take on board the new information you are delivering, over and above trusting his own instincts. Like any exercise involving handling, it should not be used too often as you don't want to make the dog sticky or over-reliant upon you to handle him.

ly conditioned in a variety of locations, the dog may not be stopping because it is over-aroused (by the retrieve or environment), or you haven't considered some of the factors we discussed in Part I (wind direction, terrain, cover), or the dog has too much initiative or self-belief, and less trust and reliance on you as its partner. Sometimes, as well as not stopping at all, the dog may only reluctantly come to a stop after some distance or after hunting on.

To improve these poor stops you need to be consistent, and be sure you remediate every time, even if it involves walking a considerable distance out to the dog to reset it. There are no shortcuts to be made here. When you do go out to your dog to put it back at the location where the whistle was blown, try not to do so with a poor attitude, and never put the lead on the dog to take it back to the spot. You don't want to send the message to your dog that the lead has a negative association or is some form of punishment. The lead should simply be a link between yourself and the dog for you to walk safely, in a 'switched off' way, from A to B. So, either call the dog to you, or go and collect it and walk with it back to where you want to reset the stop exercise. Sit or stand the dog up and then walk back to where you were originally handling from, before re-blowing the stop whistle and praising the dog as he has now got the stop exercise right. This will help cement the correct stop picture. You can then carry on from there to give the dog a further reward of the retrieve.

When trying to improve stops, benchmark what you want, and then classify the stops that the dog offers as follows, and give feedback to your dog accordingly:

- An excellent/improved stop: praise and reward. This may be strong vocal praise, or going out to the dog to give it a food reward, physical contact or a thrown ball.
- An 'adequate' stop: not worthy of praise. You don't want to endorse it, so just accept it and move on. The main thing is to notice this. Are these becoming more infrequent? This is a transition phase.
- A poor stop: remediate by resetting the dog and repeating the exercise.

CLOSING THE GAP

You can do this exercise if you know that you are going to have to go out to your dog to reset him if he isn't stopping consistently. Once you have sent your dog on a retrieve, from your side, start to follow him up so that when you blow your stop whistle you are much nearer the dog than you would be had you stayed in the same place.

This means you can be quicker to respond if he doesn't stop, if you need to reset him in place. Equally, you can be quicker to respond if he gives you an excellent stop – you can go to him immediately and reward him. Also, doing this exercise, the dog will realise that you are always there, in close proximity, rather than him being beyond any connection with you as he works at longer distances.

In the Introduction we discussed 'active listening', whereby you need to make the effort to listen to somebody talking to you and to engage with this. The same philosophy is appropriate for your dog when it is going out towards a retrieve. It is not enough for the dog just to hear a whistle cue: he needs to be running out in a receptive state, whereby he is listening out for your additional input, which can help him to succeed.

STRATEGIC HANDLING

A few final words on handling, particularly when training. It is advisable to build in handling, rather than avoiding it, even if you don't think the dog's responsiveness is as yet very good. A mistake that some people make is not to attempt to handle their dog because they are not sure how it will react. But this can become a vicious circle in that the dog is left to its own devices more, and therefore doesn't expect or want to be handled to help it pick retrieves.

Rather than trying to pick retrieves in a single cast, look for opportunities to handle the dog, sometimes multiple times, to develop its resilience to being handled for when you might need to do so. Also, think strategically about stopping and handling your dog – for example, if you know there is a bird over a rise in the ground some twenty metres out of

Take the opportunity to handle when the dog is in sight.

sight. In this case, rather than sending the dog out and then, when it is out of sight, trying to guess if it is in approximately the right area to stop and hunt, you could use a judicious stop whistle at the rise of the hill before you lose sight of it. This has two advantages: first, you have killed some of the speed of the outrun, so you can just send the dog back to the area and he will be travelling more slowly and is therefore more likely to wind the bird. Second, you can use the stop to perform a line correction in terms of ensuring the dog goes back on the correct line just downwind of the bird, rather than powering past it at full speed upwind.

The other time a strategic stop can be useful is when putting the dog into a dense wood. Again, stop the dog on the outside and put him in at right or left back so that the wind is in his favour, and so that he is travelling at a sensible pace.

Try to think ahead when you have retrieves like these, so that you plan when you will stop the dog and how you will proceed.

Also think about your handling when there are difficult obstacles to negotiate, such as a deep ditch or a dense hedge. With terrain that might challenge the dog, it is far better to handle the dog when it is in sight or when it is nearer to you. For example, in the case of a retrieve behind a hedge, any correction of line that is necessary should be done before the dog goes through the hedge, as once it is the other side it will be far more difficult to handle it successfully. Conversely, with a retrieve the other side of a deep gulley or stream, where the dog is still in sight, and with a dog that is less confident with tackling these obstacles, it is a good idea to send it over the stream or ditch at the point closest to you, and to then cast it left or right once it gets along the other side.

8 MARKING AND HUNTING ISSUES

Hunting and retrieving are generally considered to be the 'fun' part of gundog training, and the areas that shouldn't need as much concerted, formalised input if the dog has a strong working instinct. But raw talent alone will not be enough for the dog that is required to work consistently in the field, hunting for and retrieving game when requested to do so, at the right time and in the right place.

Whilst these skills are largely inherent, there is still plenty of training to do to ensure that the desired outcomes are reached. This training has to be carried out in a balanced way so that natural ability is harnessed without sacrificing the dog's innate ability to find game and solve problems for itself.

NURTURING A DOG'S PROBLEM-SOLVING CAPACITY

The role of a gundog is one of working in complete harmony with his handler, sometimes on his own initiative, be that on a marked retrieve or tracking the line on a runner, and at other times taking on board input and control without question. The ideal dog is one that is able to balance these capabilities perfectly, switching between the two modes effortlessly and without question – and it is down to you as a handler to help and guide your young dog on a path to achieving this successfully.

Give a young dog too much freedom and you may find that it is reluctant to take on board your input, or

it comes to view your intervention with resentment. Conversely, put too much control and enforced structure on to your dog and you will find that he becomes reticent and unwilling, or worried, to try behaviours on his own. It is up to you as a handler not only to understand the type of dog that you have (for example, some are more independent or confident, whilst others are perpetually seeking additional input) but also to tailor your actions and reactions accordingly when you are training.

You may often be provided with opportunities to let your youngster learn, but you have to recognise them. For example, if you are sending your dog for a mark that has fallen just over a stock fence, this is an ideal opportunity to watch how your dog relates to this challenge, if he doesn't accurately mark the precise fall over the fence. In the case where the dog stops short and begins hunting in front of the fence, the temptation is for the handler to step in fairly promptly, stopping the dog and pushing him back to ensure that he is successful in finding the retrieve.

However, in this case, although the dog has shown that he can handle, and the handler has helped him to achieve success in retrieving, the dog hasn't actually learnt much, and he hasn't been allowed the freedom to try to solve the problem for himself. What would have happened if you had allowed him to continue searching in front of the fence? What might he have done next? The chances are that he would possibly have pulled forwards to try a different area nearer, but having not succeeded in these efforts, he may well then have tried further back and taken himself over the fence. But if you continually step in too quickly, you will never know, and he will never have the opportunity to try to work out challenges on his own.

You can set up this exercise to try yourself, if your dog is relatively confident with jumping fences already. Find a stock fence with some long grass in front of it that will break the groundline, meaning that it is a little tricky to mark the precise fall of the dummy. Throw a mark well short of the fence, and send the dog for it, so that it gets used to marking and picking into this long grass but is not going over the fence. Next, throw another mark right at the base of the fence. Your dog may short-mark this one because it has had previous successes somewhat short of this fall, but give him the opportunity to work out that this dummy has fallen further back. Once this has been picked, you can then try throwing a dummy just over the fence and sending the dog once more. Watch how he relates to it. Again, he may short-mark it or hunt along the fenceline, where he won't find the dummy this time.

You can aid the dog in his learning by being mindful of the wind direction when you set up this retrieve. If you do it so that the wind direction is in his favour (towards you from the fence) this will help your dog scent the retrieve over the fence and aid him in his decision to jump over the fence to find the mark. On another occasion, set up the retrieve in reverse so the wind is not coming from the dummy towards the dog. Then you will see that the dog's decision-making process is solely problem solving in relation to where the dummy might have landed, and not because he has winded it. Standing back and watching your dog work and trying to problem solve on its own this way, rather than rushing to step in and handle it too quickly, requires some self-restraint on your part – particularly if you are a person who likes to take control.

If you are training alone, take some time just to observe in more detail some of the behaviours that your dog is offering, and notice how he is relating to the retrieves. Does he ask for support – and then you answer him? Is this becoming a pattern? Or does he become extremely independent after several

Allow the dog to work out where the dummy has landed rather than handling it on to it.

attempts at handling have broken down? Try to watch and analyse what is happening before you rush to act or react to a certain situation. I often say to students 'Leave him! What's the worst that can happen?' This is a chance to watch and really learn about your dog, and in so doing you will become better able to support him more appropriately in future training.

POOR MARKING

Teaching gundogs to 'lock on' to a mark with their eyes, so that they hold the picture of where the retrieve is in their heads, is an important process in teaching effective marking. The longer a dog can remain locked on to the mark, the better that visual picture is likely to be of where to find the retrieve, in terms of both its line and depth. Gradually extending the time that the dog stays focused on the mark before sending him will help to improve this. If he looks away before you have the chance to send him,

A dog that looks up to the handler, waiting to be sent for the retrieve, is more likely to lose its concentration on the mark.

then pick up the mark yourself (or with a helper) and reset the exercise. Next time ensure that you send him more quickly before he looks away.

People will sometimes characterise their dogs as 'poor markers' when in fact they just haven't been taught the skill-set involved in retaining the mark, or the handler hasn't noticed that the dog is building additional cues into the retrieve sequence. For example, some dogs learn that once they have looked at the retrieve they can look at their handler, and then the handler will send them for the retrieve, using a vocal command and arm signal. The dog then starts taking their focus away from the retrieve more and more quickly in anticipation of being sent.

Equally, those dogs that don't mark very well are often the ones that are handled on to their marks, and so the vicious circle starts: the dog isn't marking and so the handler helps, so the dog never learns to mark because it always receives help from his handler. If your dog has failed to mark accurately, resist the temptation to handle him in the first instance, and recall him instead and reset the mark to have another try. Using this method, the dog will be able to problem solve to see what gains him success.

OBSESSION WITH MARKS

Once you have established the ability of the dog to 'lock on' to its marks, then it is important that this does not become an overriding factor for the dog in the presence of marked retrieves. You don't want them obsessing over the mark above all else, and not being able to come away from it if required, as this will lead to additional issues.

You will, therefore, need to go through a process of ensuring the dog will 'lock off' as well. You can achieve this by doing a self-thrown mark, letting the dog watch it and stay locked on, and then send the dog. Then repeat the throw, but this time, instead of sending the dog, turn 180 degrees and heel the dog away from the mark. If your heelwork is reliable, the dog should automatically turn with you at heel and be prepared to walk in the opposite direction. You can then use this retrieve as a memory blind once you have walked away, rewarding the dog for his patience and good heelwork with you.

Mixing up this sequence of sending directly for the retrieve and walking away will help ensure that the dog understands the concept of locking on and locking off, and it means that you can mix up your retrieve work with direct marks and trailing memory blinds. It will also help with steadiness and frustration tolerance, in that the dog realises that even though he may have fulfilled your criteria to retrieve (by remaining steady, focused and quiet) he may not be sent for every retrieve, or there may be some delayed gratification (via memory blinds) involved. This will help him to manage his impulses.

HANDLER FOCUSED (SPANIEL)

Unlike retrievers, spaniels that are hunting will mark the quarry that they have flushed to be shot from a position remote from their handler, not at heel.

Sometimes in training you may find that a spaniel that is hunting in front of you as you walk up is too focused on you, watching to see what you are going to do next. This quite often happens if you train alone and throw marks or hide tennis balls for the dog: it starts to anticipate you doing this.

Also, once you begin work on handling and whistle control then this can exacerbate the problem as the dog becomes very focused on you. You will need to re-establish the scenario of your spaniel flushing the bird and then watching it fly away as it is shot, rather than looking back at you for guidance.

If your dog has this issue, go back to building a reliable 'lock on' from the heel position and ensure that this is solid. The following steps, which will help create the desired focus on marking, will necessarily involve making the dog a little unsteady again at first because you will need to send him as soon as he sees the mark go out, before he has time to take his attention away from it. This temporary loss of steadiness to flush and shot is to be expected if you

This spaniel is looking for instruction rather than maintaining its focus on the mark.

Start with the spaniel alongside you.

Then move the dog slightly in front, so it is still easy for her to retain her focus on the dummy.

Eventually the dog will be able to stay focused on the mark from the remote position.

keep sending your dog quickly for marks, but you should be able to rebuild steadiness into the regime again as you start to take more time in sending, because your dog is able to lock on to the remote mark for longer. Eventually you should be able to expect both good marking skills and steadiness to flush and fall too.

Once you have the dog marking successfully at heel, without looking away from the retrieve, you will then position him slightly in front of you, still facing away from you. From this position he is still aware of your presence but is not squarely facing you, and it is easy for him to focus on the mark rather than you. Again, send the dog promptly as soon as you throw the dummy, so there is no time for him to shift his gaze.

If the dog can successfully achieve this you will start to move him further and further away from yourself in small incremental steps. If you have a

The dog is looking back at the thrower after he has thrown the mark.

failure, whereby the dog looks back at you, then don't be concerned to go backwards again, placing the dog nearer to you, and repeating the exercise for success. If the dog looks back at you at any point, you need to walk out and pick up the dummy so that you are denying him the retrieve. There will be no reward for looking at you.

As well as moving the dog further in front of you, you can start to change his orientation. You may not yet be able to sit him squarely facing you as you throw, but you may be able to angle him one way or another. Gradually you will shift his orientation in relation to you, and you will also be able to work out where he is able to mark the best and achieve success. You can then make gradual changes that support his marking. Some dogs will have a preference as to which side is easiest for them to mark from. For example, my

spaniel is much stronger at locking on if she is facing to the right, rather than the left. This may have something to do with me throwing right-handed, or the fact that I have used my right hand as a 'stop sign' out of habit (being right-handed). Or it may be that she is inherently right-sided (*see* Chapter 2). So the left-facing marks for her needed a little more work.

LOOKING AT THE REMOTE THROWER

Looking at the remote thrower is a similar issue to the dog that is taking its focus off the mark to ask the handler to send it. It is locking off, but in this case the dog watches the mark thrown and then looks back at the thrower again (usually in anticipation of them throwing another mark, as this has become a pattern).

The thrower initially stands alongside the handler and dog, so as not to appear in their line of sight.

Then the thrower will move forwards so that they are in the dog's peripheral vision.

The dog has retained its focus on the mark and not looked back towards the thrower.

If the dog has taken part in several group training sessions, he will soon learn that all retrieves will come from the remote thrower, and that is why he will turn his gaze back that way, losing the current mark.

The solution to this issue is similar to what has been described above regarding the spaniel that has lost its mark. However, in this case you will ask a thrower to come and work with you, at first alongside you and then gradually moving them further into the picture.

First, have the helper stand alongside you and your dog and throw a mark out. If your dog locks on to it, then you should send him for this mark. This will set a successful pattern. Your dog won't look back at the thrower in this instance as they are alongside you and not in your dog's field of vision. Next you can ask the thrower to move one pace further forwards, so that they start to enter the dog's overall picture of the mark, but are only incrementally inside it. Again, if the dog remains locked on to the mark, then send him for this retrieve.

Gradually you will ask the thrower to move further forwards so they move more into the picture. All the time monitor how your dog relates to the thrower once they have thrown the mark, and if the dog takes his gaze away from the dummy and back to the thrower then you need to backtrack again. The dog should only be sent for the mark if he remains steady and focused on it.

You will need to proof this activity by eventually asking the thrower not only to move forwards, but also left or right in the dog's field of vision. Carefully watch your dog when it marks as it is not always easy to see a dog subtly moving its gaze from the dummy back to the thrower. Some dogs will just move their eyes rather than their whole head.

While you are working on this issue, only work on single marks, so that the dog gets into a pattern of seeing a mark and being sent for it. The problem described is usually one that has been created through throwing multiple marks and the dog getting

Hesitating before picking, asking permission from their handler, constitutes standing over game.

used to looking at the thrower wanting another to be thrown. So breaking this cycle is an important part of dealing with the issue.

STANDING OVER GAME

Those who compete, or aspire to compete, in field trials, particularly in the UK, may have heard the expression 'standing over game' and understand that this is deemed to be a major fault in a competing gundog. But there is not a lot of consensus sometimes as to whether a dog has actually stood over game, so the term requires some clarification.

When people talk about standing over game, they mean that the dog has found the bird but instead of picking it up directly and returning to their handler, they hesitate over it, sometimes looking at it and then looking back at the handler.

What Is It (and What Isn't It)?

It is easiest to start with what isn't 'standing over game'. Stopping a dog on the whistle when it is next to a bird is not standing over game: that is just poor timing (or good timing, depending on how you look at it!). There is a world of difference between standing over game and honouring a stop whistle, and a good judge should be able to distinguish the difference easily.

Most judges would not penalise a dog in this situation for honouring a stop whistle, as long as the dog then went on to pick the bird without hesitation. It may, at worst, merit a comment in the book describing what had happened, in case this was a regular pattern of events with other retrieves – in which case it would be worthy of discussion with co-judges.

When dogs are being trained to a high standard, they are expected to honour stop whistles, sometimes in the most distracting conditions. A good dog is able to achieve this reliably so that it hears the whistle and stops without question. It would be undesirable to have a dog that sometimes acknowledges a stop whistle and at other times decides not to do so. Having a dog that is reliably trained on the stop whistle is mostly a huge asset.

However, putting the use of a whistle aside, if a dog puts its head down to pick game and then lifts it up to ask permission to pick, then that is standing over game. Or if a dog reaches game and hesitates over it (acknowledging it) before deciding to pick it, then that would also be classed as standing over game.

It is not always clear whether a dog has stood over game, especially if it is working in cover.

The spaniel should stay within range to enable the gun to shoot what is flushed.

No handler cues have been issued, and the dog has made the decision to stand over the game on its own.

In deciding whether a dog has stood over game, a judge should have a full understanding of dog work, as well as considering the terrain and conditions of the day. For example, is the dog actually trying to pull the bird out of very dense cover or a heavy bog? Or is the dog standing on the cock pheasant's tail, whilst trying to pick it? Only if a judge has moved into a position to see the dog picking clearly, is she or he able to make such a decision. If the dog appears to take a long time gathering game, but the judge is unable to see exactly what is happening, then she or he should not penalise the dog, but instead

must give it the benefit of the doubt, and ensure that they are in a better place to view the dog working on its next retrieve.

What Causes Standing Over Game?

The primary cause for standing over game is usually a pattern of behaviour that the dog has learnt (think of these as 'cues' to retrieve). For example, the dog is sent out on a retrieve, which may be either a mark or blind, and when it reaches the area it is requested to 'hunt' by the handler with a whistle or voice cue. This becomes a pattern, so that every time the dog goes out it hears the hunt command when it is in the area of the retrieve, and after that it picks the bird. The dog recognises the sequence of events and eventually understands that it only picks the bird once it has heard the hunt cue. This can lead to the dog locating the bird, but waiting to hear the hunt cue before it picks it up.

Depending on the nature of the dog, other subsidiary factors can be over-reliance on the handler before performing any task – usually caused by a handler controlling the dog too much in all its work, and the dog not being allowed to work for itself – and subsequent worry or concern by the dog.

In addition, repeatedly blowing the stop whistle as the dog scents the bird can also lead to it sticking and standing over game, as it is learning a pattern of stopping (firstly on the whistle, and later without the whistle) once it touches scent. To avoid this, the handler needs to know where the game is located precisely, and only intervene with a stop whistle when it is 'safe' to do so – for example, when the dog is in an upwind position and unable to scent the game.

Rectifying the Issue

How you deal with a dog potentially standing over game will depend on whether you are in a competition situation or just training. If you are competing, you are dealing with 'damage limitation' and management, whereas when you are training you are looking at creating good habits rather than bad ones.

In competition, be vigilant, and if you do inadvertently stop the dog as it indicates on scent (you should be able to see this through its body language) and goes to pick, then roll your stop whistle immediately into a hunt whistle so that the dog is supported to carry on hunting and picking without hesitation.

In training, continue to practise stop whistles and adherence to them in all situations, keeping the cue separate to the hunt whistle. You still want to have a dog that stops reliably on the whistle whether it has winded something or not, but take care not to set up a habit of stopping the dog every time it has touched scent. Rather, look for opportunities to stop the dog out of the area of the retrieve, away from any scent, before moving it into the area to work freely on its own.

NETTLE: ASKING TOO MANY QUESTIONS

Four-year-old Labrador Nettle was extremely biddable and loved working with her handler Jim. Her response to the whistle and his handling cues were very good, and she enjoyed working with him to find her retrieves. However, when he cued her to hunt an area, she would only hunt for a few seconds before stopping and looking back at him for reassurance and further instruction. Jim found this frustrating, but was at a loss as to how to deal with it in a dog that was in all other respects fully trained.

When Nettle stopped like this he had tried shouting at her 'Find it, find it!' in frustration, and she had responded to this by getting on with hunting again – but this wasn't a long-term solution, and ultimately it was prolonging the issue as she was still asking for this input, which he was readily giving.

Jim's goal was to prolong the time that Nettle hunted without asking for further input, and ultimately to eliminate the habit altogether. He had tried to build this up with longer durations of hunting before she found the retrieve, and he ignored her when she looked at him. I suggested trying the opposite approach to this, only asking her to hunt for short bursts with almost immediate success. This built up her confidence in her own ability, and she regained her passion for hunting.

As well as doing this, I suggested we introduce an element of competition into the equation, to help promote her desire to hunt. So we took Jim's other two dogs out with us at the same time, putting them all in the designated hunt area and letting them see us throw a couple of balls into the long grass there. They then knew there was something to find. We moved away from the three dogs, leaving them remotely, then gave them a stop whistle cue to get their attention focused on us, and then a hunt whistle cue, when they all started to hunt frantically to pick the balls before one of the others could pick one. This became a game that Jim could play with these dogs periodically to improve Nettle's desire to hunt. She started to hunt more aggressively and vigorously so as not to be beaten to the find by one of the other dogs.

For the times when Jim didn't have another dog with him, I also suggested he try doing some 'collaborative hunting' with Nettle whereby he put the ball into the long grass and then stayed with her. He then asked her to hunt, and whilst she was doing this, he joined in looking for the ball too. Doing this took away some of the formality of the exercise and made it a fun and engaging game that they could play together. Sometimes Nettle would find the ball, to much praise from Jim, and at other times Jim would find it himself with much excitement!

Once a new habit of hunting without 'popping' (the dog stopping and asking questions) had been established, on these short hunts and during the fun games, it gave both Nettle and Jim more confidence. They were then able to move on to gradually prolonging the duration of the hunting before a find.

The competition of other dogs can be a great way to encourage a reluctant hunter or one lacking in confidence.

HUNTING TOO FAR AND WIDE

One of the most common issues with hunting, with both retrievers and spaniels, is the dog that takes in too much ground, ranging when it hunts. That is, it is hunting usually too far out and racing across the ground rather than working over it in a methodical, systematic way. A fast dog can look very stylish and will often be remarked upon, but if it is not actually locating game it isn't much use. It is better to have a dog with less speed but a more methodical approach, which will work the ground fully and produce the game efficiently.

Retrievers Ranging too Far

If your retriever is moving too far when requested to hunt and not holding a sensible area, then you have two options. You can use the attrition approach, whereby you put the dog into the desired area and use your hunt cue to ask it to hunt. If it moves out of the area, then you can watch it and wait, and only re-cue it to hunt when it is in the area again. The philosophy behind this method is that you are telling the dog where to hunt, and if it does so where you ask it to, then it will be successful. But if it hunts elsewhere then that is wasted effort, and it won't get any success from it. For some dogs this makes sense, and they quickly realise that you have valuable information to impart, and that as a team you will find things together.

However, for other dogs – those that just enjoy the act of hunting more so than locating the retrieve – then this method is unlikely to be successful as it just gives them 'carte blanche' to go off hunting wherever they please. For this sort of dog it is best to walk out and reset them in the desired area and start again, issuing the cue in the correct area. You may need to simplify things and let the dog see you placing something in the given area to ensure that it understands that it will be worthwhile for it to hold a tight area in order to find.

Spaniel Pulling Forwards

When your spaniel is hunting in front of you to locate and flush game, you want it to hold a methodical pattern and cover the ground appropriately, checking out all areas of cover, and staying within range of the gun that will be shooting. However, as the season progresses, it is likely that your dog will become wise to the fact that game is often running on ahead, and it may well start to 'pull' you by moving too far forwards and pulling out of range. If this starts to occur, the tendency can be for the handler to try to rush to keep up with the dog, and before you know it you are having to chase your dog through the wood just to stay near it.

This pattern needs addressing, and there are a number of ways you can improve the situation. One is to stand still rather than keep walking, and see if your dog realises that you are not just following him. If so, you can recall him and start again, or you can go out and get him and start the hunting pattern from where you stopped. This will show the dog that pulling forwards means no progress, and actually has the reverse outcome, with hunting being curtailed. It needs patience and consistency to do properly so the dog understands what is happening.

Another method you can try is walking backwards and sideways occasionally to encourage the dog to watch you and become more aware of his proximity to you. In this manner you are opening up the distance between you and making your dog check where he is and monitor his range.

In addition, go back to re-establishing the boundaries of your hunt pattern by using your turn whistle just before the dog gets to where you consider the optimum range to be. Use this turn whistle to change the dog's direction before it goes too far in each direction. Whilst it would be noisy to do this consistently when working, you will only be doing this for a period of time while you re-establish the correct parameters. You should then be able to revert to the dog turning automatically as it reaches the edge of this newly reinforced pattern.

RETRIEVER 'STICKINESS' ON HUNTING

Whilst hunting under control in a defined area is desirable, having a dog that asks too many questions when hunting is not. You want the dog to get on with the job he has been asked to do in the area, with minimal additional handler input. Some dogs become so controlled in their work that when they are given free rein to hunt an area for lost game they can become overly needy and keep stopping or 'popping', effectively asking their handler if they are doing right and wanting the hunt cue to be reissued. This is frustrating and unnecessary if the dog has learnt what the hunt cue means in the first place, which is to get on and hunt that piece of ground to locate game. But some handlers are at a loss as to what to do when the dog stops, looks at them and asks them for more input, and many will just reissue the hunt cue to make the dog carry on – which then feeds the cycle of the dog 'puppeting' the handler for more input.

The important thing is to break this cue-response cycle and reset it into a new pattern, and to do this by setting things up for early success for the dog (*see* box on previous spread).

CONCLUSION

Life would pall if it were all sugar; salt is bitter if taken by itself; but when tasted as part of the dish, it savours the meat. Difficulties are the salt of life.

ROBERT BADEN-POWELL

Life is inevitably peppered with imperfections and difficulties, and gundog training is no different in this respect. As we discussed in Chapter 1, there are many mistakes that can be made along the way – mostly by ourselves rather than our dogs. You should accept this and endeavour to learn from these mistakes, using the experience that comes out of them to inform future behaviour.

As George Santayana said in *The Life of Reason* (1905): 'Those who cannot remember the past are condemned to repeat it.' It is important to use the lessons of the past, but to use them wisely. The more dogs you train the more experience you will gain. However, once you have had an issue with one dog, there is a tendency to not want to 'make the same mistake twice'. This is logical in one sense, in that you will have greater experience now, so you will not repeat some of the behaviours that may have led to this problem. However, you also need to remember that no two dogs will be completely alike, even with similar breeding. Therefore ensuring that you proceed extra steadily with your new dog because your last dog was so hot-headed may be completely inappropriate. This dog might need encouraging to run in, with no control, because it lacks drive or confidence. It is likely to need a different approach. You will still have your acquired knowledge from the previous dog, but knowing when, and if, to apply it will be the art in progressing successfully.

CORE SKILLS RECAP

What will have become apparent to you as you have worked through *Gundog SOS* is that the majority of the issues outlined in Part II have their roots embedded in the core foundation skills, such as recall, stays and heelwork. A lack of attention to detail in getting these basic elements right in early training will mean that your house is likely to come tumbling down again in the future.

With an older dog, it is harder to remedy established problems. In this case you will need to accept that it is sometimes necessary to go back to go forwards. This will pay dividends in the long term. If you have hit an issue with a dog that you would regard as experienced, set about writing down the main elements that are letting down some of the more advanced processes, and work out a way of focusing on these in dedicated short training sessions. Isolating individual elements in the chain of behaviour is an excellent way of putting more focus on the areas that need the most work. Once you have achieved progress and improved the problem element, you can then piece the chain of behaviours back together again and move on.

BE ADAPTABLE

The definition of insanity is said to be doing the same thing over and over again but expecting a different outcome. If you want change to happen then you have to be prepared to modify your behaviour and be flexible. Sometimes it is hard to break old habits, though, particularly if they have been successful in the past. Once you have developed your own methods for achieving certain core skills then it is difficult to consider abandoning or altering them.

When I acquired Twig and started to try to line her up for memory blind retrieves, it was very 'hit and miss'. Her focus was not always there, and she would run out swinging her head back and forth. I have a very distinctive way of sending my dogs, whereby I bring my arm from above them and then the dog will start to track this in the air, look at my hand momentarily, and then project their gaze from my hand to where I am pointing on the horizon. Watching my dogs do this, I am then assured that they have a strong focal point in the distance and will run to this. However, this method did not work at all for Twig. If there was a visual target, she would pick this out herself and run to it. My arm cue did not appear to have any relevance. And if there wasn't a visible feature, or shot fired, then when I put my arm out, she would just scan outwards and move her head around, not settling on to any particular point to focus, and not using my arm as any sort of reference. I tried consolidating and reinforcing my arm cues in this respect over many months, but I never succeeded in her being able to pick up the arm coming from above, track it and then drop her gaze to the distance. She just couldn't relate to it.

Eventually I realised that it was time to change my method of sending so that it was easier for her to understand what was required. What had worked for many of my other dogs was not effective in this case. I have now developed a different cue for send-away with Twig alone, whereby I bring my hand up from underneath and alongside her head. For some reason this is far more acceptable to her, and she is a lot more focused in her attention relating to where my hand is pointing. It may be that her previous owner lined her up in this manner, or it may be that she just needed a different set of cues. Either way, it has reminded me to treat every dog according to its needs. Train the dog in front of you, don't just train the way you have always trained.

In this respect, it falls to us as trainers to try to be more like a sponge than a rock. Adapt and be willing to take on new thoughts and processes. Try new ideas – they might prove illuminating – and don't stay set in old ways just because you have always done it like that. By the same token, 'reading' the dog is of great importance here, in understanding what is happening and helping them to progress. Time spent just observing your dogs, and even filming them for review later, is never wasted. It is often illuminating to just watch how they react and interact, with the environment, with other dogs and with you.

All dogs will develop at different rates. And whilst the general rule of thumb is to take things steadily, not missing out on any important information or processes along the way, it is also as much a mistake to hold a bright dog back when it needs to be given more mental stimulation as it is to rush on with a youngster that clearly isn't ready.

REVEL IN THE PROCESS

Having a so-called 'difficult dog' can teach you to focus on the process of your training journey together, rather than on any eventual outcome. Your current dog might not 'go all the way' in terms of becoming a field trial champion or a reliable companion in the shooting field, but there is still an immense amount of enjoyment to be had from outings together with your gundog, working on elements of training. While there will inevitably be frustrations, trying to make gradual improvements over time should be an enjoyable challenge for you both. You will only have a relatively small number of dogs in your life, so it is important to savour the unique relationship that you have with each one. The path that you take together will not always be straightforward, and it is likely that you will have difficult decisions to make along the way. Sometimes you will choose to continue forwards, sometimes you will need to go backwards or change tack. And at other times, you will just decide to go home, have a cup of tea and try again another time! Everyone can have a bad day, and the same

Enjoy the process of training your dog and the unique bond that will form between you.

goes for dogs. This may be down to how you are both feeling, physically and mentally, or it may be due to environmental factors that you need to consider.

Rather than becoming overly goal-oriented, spend time confirming your values and priorities in gundog training. If you find it is necessary to set goals, set them small and set them achievable. Also try to understand whether you are goal setting for personal growth, or whether you are searching for external validation. The latter is often transient, whereas training in line with your values, and achieving an internal sense of accomplishment, is more fulfilling in the long run.

BIBLIOGRAPHY

CHAPTER 1

Duckworth, A. *Grit: The power of passion and perseverance* (Scribner/Simon & Schuster, 2016).

Mackesy, C. *The Boy, the Mole, the Fox and the Horse* (Ebury Press, 2019).

CHAPTER 2

Ahern, G. and Schwartz, G. 'Differential lateralization for positive versus negative emotion', *Neuropsychologia* (17(6), 693–698, 1979).

Barnard, S. et al. 'Laterality as a Predictor of Coping Strategies in Dogs Entering a Rescue Shelter', Animal Behaviour Centre, Queen's University Belfast (2018).

Batt, L. et al. 'Factors associated with success in guide dog training', *Journal of Veterinary Behavior* (3(4), 143–151, 2008).

Batt, L. et al. 'The relationships between motor lateralization, salivary cortisol concentrations and behavior in dogs', *J. Vet. Behav. Clin. Appl. Res.* (4, 216–222, 2009).

Coren, S. https://www.psychologytoday.com/gb/blog/canine-corner/201303/which-emotions-do-dogs-actually-experience (2013).

Kujala, M. 'Canine emotions as seen through human social cognition', *Animal Sentience* (14 (1), 2017).

Laverack, K. et al. 'The effect of sex and age on paw use within a large sample of dogs *(Canis familiaris)*', *Applied Animal Behaviour Science* (238, Article 105298, 2021).

Marshall-Pescini, S. et al. 'The effect of preferential paw usage on dogs' *(Canis familiaris)* performance in a manipulative problem-solving task', *Behavioural Processes* (100, 40–43, 2013).

Mayer, E., *The Mind-Gut Connection* (HarperCollins, 2016).

Mills, D. et al. 'Pain and problem behaviour in cats and dogs', *Animals* (10(2), 318, 2020) https://doi.org/10.3390/ani10020318

Ocklenburg, S. and Gunturkun, O. *The Lateralized Brain: The Neuroscience and Evolution of Hemispheric Asymmetries* (Academic Press, 2017).

Papadatou-Pastou, M. et al. 'Human handedness: A meta-analysis', *Psychological Bulletin* (146, 481–524, 2020).

Rife D.C. 'Handedness, with Special Reference to Twins', *Genetics* (25, 178-186, 1940).

Scales, S. *Retriever Training* (Swan Hill Press, 1992).

Siniscalchi, M. et al. 'Dogs turn left to emotional stimuli', *Behavioural Brain Research* (208: 516–521, 2010).

Tomkins, L. et al. 'First-stepping Test as a measure of motor laterality in dogs *(Canis familiaris)*', *Journal of Veterinary Behavior Clinical Applications and Research* (5(5):247–255, 2010).

CHAPTER 3

Roberts, M. *The Horses in my Life* (Headline, 2004).

CHAPTER 4

Kross, E. *Chatter: The Voice in Our Head and How to Harness It* (Vermilion, 2022).

Martin, S. & Friedman, S. 'The Power of Trust', presented at the IAATE Conference (2013).

Tackman, A. et al. 'Depression, negative emotionality, and self-referential language: A multi-lab, multi-measure, and multi-language-task research synthesis', *Journal of Personality and Social Psychology* (116(5), 817–834, 2019).

Wang, Y. et al. 'Early-career setback and future career impact', *Nature Communications* (10, 4331, 2019).

CHAPTER 5

Menzies, J. *Training the Working Spaniel* (Quiller, 2010).

CONCLUSION

Santayana, G. *The Life of Reason* (1905).

INDEX

ACKNOWLEDGEMENTS

Thank you to all my training friends and colleagues who have been with me on this journey. We have had countless ups and downs together, with a variety of dogs, all of which have enriched our overall experience. Thanks also go to all the students whom I have mentored. I have enjoyed watching your dogs develop and learn, and in turn, you have helped me to broaden my own knowledge and skill set.

I am greatly indebted to Pip Wheatcroft, who provided so many of the photos for my first book, *Advanced Retriever Training*, and this time has played a pivotal role working patiently with me to produce the vast majority of the photos to bring my text to life in *Gundog SOS*. We've also enjoyed training our litter siblings together. I quite simply could not have done this without her. Other photo contributions have kindly come from ACME Whistles, Jill Gardiner, Sarah Middleton, Pete Riches and Vicki Ruston.

Thanks go again to Karen and Colin Rodger at Bern Pet Foods, who continue to support me and ensure that my team of dogs at Stauntonvale Gundogs get the very best nutrition to keep them in peak physical condition. With strong bodies come healthy minds.

And thank you to my husband Derek for tolerating all the inevitable ups and downs that life with working gundogs throws at us daily. We have had, and continue to have, an amazing team of dogs in our lives, and we are both far richer for it – although our bank manager may disagree!

First published in 2024 by
The Crowood Press Ltd
Ramsbury
Marlborough
Wiltshire SN8 2HR

enquiries@crowood.com
www.crowood.com

© Laura Hill 2024

British Library Cataloguing-in-Publication Data
A catalogue record for this book is available from the British Library.
ISBN 978 0 7198 4345 7

Typeset by surichardsgraphicdesign.com
Cover design by surichardsgraphicdesign.com

Printed and bound in China by Printworks Global

ADVANCED
RETRIEVER
TRAINING

Laura Hill